Advance Praise For
Learn The Secrets

Tell me there's a job tougher than a pharmaceutical sales rep's and I'll tell you that you've never spent a day with one. And it's only getting tougher as today's reps are challenged not only by their human competitors in the field, but an alphabet soup of restrictions that will continue to test the determination and intellect of even the most hardy contenders. With their astute rundown of the implications of HIPAA and PhRMA, OIG and ACCME on pharmaceutical sales and marketing, Kaputa and Zimmerman reveal the key to success in this dynamic and rewarding job: Stay informed and be prepared. That isn't as easy as it sounds, but their book is a good start.

Sibyl Shalo, **Senior Editor**
Pharmaceutical Executive Magazine

The book challenges the rep to become the "Value Added" for the doctor. This isn't often found in scripted verbatims and canned sales training. Approaching a doctor from the perspective of going above and beyond what the doctor expects can differentiate a rep. For example, when doctors contract with managed care, many of these contract engagements are tenuous and tense. If a rep could help a medical practice become valuable to a health plan, that's value-added.

Bill Trombetta, **Professor of Pharmaceutical Strategy/Marketing**
Executive Pharmaceutical Marketing MBA Programs,
St. Joseph's University, Philadelphia, PA

As a practicing physician the "SMART" advice provided in "Learn The Secrets" goes a long way toward helping sales reps learn to be an advocate for their busy physician clients. The time drug reps spend in the physician's office should be valued—"Learn The Secrets" provides a framework to develop that valued relationship.

Vincent Esposito, **MD, New York, NY**

D1036573

The Combat-Ready Guide is a valuable guide to delivering a competitive edge for an individual trying to break in or wanting to sustain an advantage in the aggressive pharmaceutical sales field. The authors put the practical issues of day-to-day responsibilities within the broader framework of the need for long-term and resourceful self-management practices for maximizing rep contribution to the bottom line. The insights and suggestions have been great talking points in my advisory and teaching capacity for both my undergraduate and graduate students in the pharmaceutical marketing major at Saint Joseph's University. I highly recommend this book as a most useful and definitive "quick" read and reference text.

Carolyn Choh Fleming, **Professor, Pharmaceutical Marketing Saint Joseph's University, Philadelphia, PA**

Turn yourself from foe to friend in five minutes. Fabulous, fast, and fascinating…a "Must Read" for reps who want to succeed with busy doctors.

Henry Fishman, MD, **Washington D.C.**

The chapters on the pharmaceutical industry, the clinical process and how to present pharmaceutical sales pieces are a must read for job candidates trying to break into pharmaceutical sales. Knowledge of the industry including the buzzwords will not only make you look smart, it will help you stand out from the crowd. In today's competitive job market, that's an important edge to have.

Sandra Evans, **PhD, Executive Director, Clinical Operations, Forest Labs**

This book should be mandatory reading not only for people trying to land a job as a pharmaceutical sales rep, but also for everyone on the commercial side of the pharma business so that they know the importance of our frontline soldiers, the sales representatives. It would make my job easier because I would know that the candidates who have read this book are of the caliber that I want to represent. The book really says it all.

Shellie Caplan, **President Caplan Associates**

If you are looking for a helpful, insightful how-to guide on breaking into pharmaceutical sales, this book is for you. It tells it like it is, plus it's a fun read.

R.L., **pharmaceutical sales rep, Orlando, FL**

THIS BOOK IS NOW MY BIBLE.

D.S., **pharmaceutical sales rep, San Diego, CA**

I wish I had this book when I broke into the business. You'll find the pharma buzzwords, sample exercises and role-plays extremely helpful as you prepare for interviews. You'll be ten steps ahead of the other job candidates.

K.B., **pharmaceutical sales rep, New York, NY**

Learn The Secrets

Learn The Secrets

The Field-Tested, Combat-Ready Guide To Becoming A Pharmaceutical Sales Representative

Includes The New Guidelines, Sample Sales Pieces And Practice Role-Plays Every Job Candidate Should Know About

Catherine Kaputa
and
Lynn Zimmerman

iUniverse, Inc.
New York   Lincoln   Shanghai

Learn The Secrets
The Field-Tested, Combat-Ready Guide To Becoming A Pharmaceutical
Sales Representative

iUniverse books may be ordered through booksellers or by contacting:

iUniverse
2021 Pine Lake Road, Suite 100
Lincoln, NE 68512
www.iuniverse.com
1-800-Authors (1-800-288-4677)

Book jacket designed by Laura Berkowitz Gilbert

ISBN-13: 978-0-595-34164-1 (pbk)
ISBN-13: 978-0-595-78934-4 (ebk)
ISBN-10: 0-595-34164-0 (pbk)
ISBN-10: 0-595-78934-X (ebk)

Printed in the United States of America

To Mom and Dad, for believing in me

To my clients, for unending inspiration

To Mike and Ramsey, for life itself

CK

To my parents, for a lifetime of encouragement

To my managers, for my professional development

To Jim, for enriching my life

LZ

Contents

Preface

So? Why are you interested in pharmaceutical sales?

If you're like most people (and you're honest with yourself), you have images of the good life dancing in your head.

True or false? The fact of the matter is most people are attracted to this specialized area of selling because they think it's a great MAP for their future: money, autonomy and perks.

And it is! Most pharmaceutical sales reps earn good money and love the industry. They love the autonomy of the job and they love selling to their highly intelligent target audience: doctors and other health care providers.

You may have gotten interested in becoming a drug rep because you saw one call on your doctor while you were in the waiting room. And if you're like most of us, you probably thought, "Gee, I can do that. What an easy life," as the sales rep breezed in, chatted briefly with the doctor and left some samples behind. For the most part, reps work alone every day and nobody knows where they are any given moment. You might see the rep bring lunch to the staff or a delivery service dropping the lunch off for the rep. It looks easy and glamorous to many people.

In the land of sales professionals, there is a hierarchy to the various types of sales jobs. The pharmaceutical sales rep is at the top of the heap (as opposed to the used car salesman who is at the bottom). There is a certain status to being a pharmaceutical sales rep. It is a wonderful job with fabulous training and experiences, but the actual job is not at all like the carefree perception you have.

Sure, there is money, autonomy and perks. But, you are running your own business in a sense, making many day-to-day decisions. You are accountable for everything that goes on in your territory—good and not so good. For the most part, your managers will not be that interested in where you are every minute of the day. But, if your market share is not moving in the right direction (up), your manager will want to know how you are spending your time.

Unlike selling a computer or copier, you don't leave any office with a signed contract for a certain number of prescriptions. So, you don't know what level of sales you are generating in your territory on a day-to-day basis. You may think you're doing a great job, but the sales data you receive may tell a different story. In general, you get market share data every three months, so you may be in a constant state of catch-up. Prescribers (rep jargon for doctors and health care providers who write prescriptions) who tell you they are writing prescriptions for your product, may not be. But, you don't really know that. You only know what they tell you.

As a pharmaceutical sales representative, you'll need to think smart. You'll need to constantly analyze your data to determine if you are spending the right amount of time and energy on the right prescribers. If you work as part of a sales team or "cluster" you may need to consult with your teammates and get their buy in to make any new strategies or sales approaches work effectively.

When you leave the field at 5:00 pm your day is not over. You have to check email and voice mail, input your calls and transmit the data to the home office via your laptop. Oops! Your laptop is out for service and won't be back for ten days. A nice break, you think? Maybe, but when it comes back, you have ten days worth of emails, reports and sales calls to catch up on.

You may be studying for the launch of a new drug or a new indication for a drug you are already selling. And you'll be tested online. You have to stay current with the ever-changing industry trends and regulations. (You are tested on the new trends and regulations as well.) You'll have reports to write and submit to your manager. All this is done at night or on weekends.

Sometimes, you'll be out at night attending education programs after you have made the required sales calls during the day. (This could make it a 14-hour day). You'll also be traveling away from home for training and sales meetings.

So, there are a lot of unseen duties and responsibilities that comes with the "MAP" and status of a pharmaceutical sales career. You need to be ready to live and breathe this job. And if you are, you can achieve success and personal career fulfillment which will bring with it all the fancy benefits you may have heard about and want!

Introduction

Getting your first job as a pharmaceutical sales representative is like going into battle. You'll need a strategy and a plan of attack. You'll need to recruit allies to help you make inroads in the industry. You'll forge powerful emotional bonds with some of your fellow recruits who are trying to break into the business. You'll get some battle scars along the way, particularly after a fifth round interview before a panel of pharmaceutical sales executives. (That's why we call it, *The Field-Tested, Combat-Ready Guide to Becoming a Pharmaceutical Sales Representative.*)

Once you do land the job, it is well worth the time, energy and struggle you may have incurred to get there. The pharmaceutical industry is a dynamic global business that offers tremendous rewards, the financial kind as well as immense personal satisfaction.

So you're probably wondering, "Are there secrets to landing this job? If so, what are they? What makes one candidate stand out from another?" Well, all those questions will be answered in this book. You will learn the answers to:

- ❖ What are pharmaceutical companies looking for?
- ❖ What are the buzzwords in the pharmaceutical industry?
- ❖ What do I need to know to look smart on interviews?
- ❖ What is the best way to go about the job hunt?
- ❖ What can I do to make my resume stand out?
- ❖ How can I make my background attractive to a hiring manager?
- ❖ What's this I hear about a brag book? Do I really need one? What do I put in it?
- ❖ How can I prepare for the interview?
- ❖ What's this I hear about group interviews?
- ❖ What's detailing? What do I do if I'm asked to present a detail piece?
- ❖ What are the new regulations governing sales representatives?
- ❖ What might I be called on to sell from in an interview?
- ❖ What is the job really like and how can I be successful at it?

You'll learn all this and much more. *Learn The Secrets* is a how-to and a how-to think book for anyone who wants to land that first job in pharmaceutical sales. It is a field guide incorporating tales and lessons learned from successful candidates written by Catherine Kaputa and Lynn Zimmerman, a career coach and a pharmaceutical sales trainer and consultant.

You'll get the inside scoop—the secrets and hidden rules of success that you need to know to break into pharmaceutical sales. You'll learn lots of practical tips and smart strategies for breaking into this industry, but you'll also learn the mindset you need to adopt to be successful. *Learn The Secrets* is for pharmaceutical sales job seekers of all stripes who want to know what they need to do to market themselves and get a job offer. It will show how you can maximize the potential of your most important asset—*You*.

1.

Take Charge Of Your Job Quest And Your Most Important Asset, *You*

> "It's nice work if you can get it.
> And you can get it if you try."
>
> —*Ira Gershwin*

The single most important asset you have is *you*. In a sense, it is your only asset. Successful people realize that success is created, and you need to adopt that attitude if you want to succeed in launching your dream career in pharmaceutical sales.

For many of us, a dream career is something that we want to happen, but we aren't ready to do what it takes to create the result. Knowing that your dream is a career in pharmaceutical sales is important, but it doesn't mean anything if you don't act on it. Most of us wouldn't leave on a trip without a game plan for the holiday. Yet, many of us coast along in our careers without too much thought as to where we are heading and what we are accomplishing. Many of us don't know how to head in a different direction. Or we give up way too soon without a good effort.

What we have found in our workshops with all types of clients is that if you truly want it and are willing to take action, you can break into pharmaceutical sales. If you do the right things, it is attainable.

Maybe a few people accomplish this goal intuitively or organically or during REM sleep, but most of us need a strategy and game plan for making it happen. This book will give you the secrets and strategies to make your dream job in pharmaceutical sales come true. But first you need to begin with the right attitude.

Secret: Think Like A Brand

The mindset that is necessary for success today in breaking into pharmaceutical sales is to think like a "brand." You need to develop the mindset of a brand manager or business owner who wants to build his product or company into a winning brand. Looking at yourself this way will help you maximize the value of the assets, resources and experience you have.

Branding shows you how to look at yourself as a product in a competitive framework. It teaches you how to differentiate that product—*you*—from the competition. The competition, of course, is all the other people vying for the job you want. When you think like a brand, you'll approach the job search differently. Branding shows you how to target a market, so you can position yourself so that you will be appealing to hiring managers at pharmaceutical companies.

You'll learn that you'll get more interest by thinking not in terms of what you want to say and do, but to flip it, and think in terms of the reaction you want from your target market, and what you have to do to get that reaction. Branding also gives you a template for developing a marketing program with specific tactics and brand messages to maximize success with the target market.

Branding for people is about finding your USP, your Unique Selling Proposition: what's different, what's relevant, and something more—the value added—that something special that sets you apart from others and helps you be more successful. Throughout this book we'll help you focus on developing a compelling reason why a pharmaceutical company should hire you and not the next person on the interview list.

You need to "package" yourself so that you are appealing, both in how you look and what kind of background you have. You need to give people a concrete reason why you are the right person for the job (your brand message.) Personal branding also means developing a strategy and game plan for reaching your dream. You need to work smarter than the others competing for the job you want.

It may sound like a lot. But it is attainable. You can do it. It starts with developing the right mental attitude. The chart below shows the difference between your old way of thinking and the new personal brand mindset we'll be talking about.

Personal Brand Mindset	vs.	Employee Mindset
Working for yourself		Working for boss
Internal security		External security
Marketing Plan		Resume
Markets		Clients, Coworkers, Management
Differentiating		Fitting in
Strategy		Working hard
Relationships		Transactions
Network		Solo
Long term		Short term

If you adopt a branding mindset, you'll also respond to changes in the marketplace. (And it's always changing.) Many of us keep doing the same things long after it is not working anymore. Personal branding is about playing an active role in your career life, and learning how to position yourself and market yourself to maximum advantage.

When we take you through this journey into pharmaceutical sales, we want to help you be successful in your career, represented by money, fame, self-esteem or whatever other measure is important to you. But we are also talking about becoming who you were meant to become, success in terms of becoming who you truly are.

The trick to being successful in your job quest is to devise a strategy that works well with the hiring managers in pharmaceutical sales and the company culture you're exploring but also is true to you—that brings more of *you* into the equation. You need to find the right fit for you.

For example, when we asked one pharmaceutical manager what he was looking for when interviewing, he told us, "I'm always looking to raise the bar of my team. I want to bring together a group of individuals with varying strengths that will build a strong team." This is very common, so it is a smart strategy to highlight specific skills and strengths or capabilities that are less expected or less commonplace.

Secret: Turn Your Experience And Strengths Into Assets For A Pharmaceutical Sales Career

Each of us is unique, with a brain, strengths and experiences that are powerful assets. Anything you have ever done or thought about can be an asset. If you think it is an asset, it is. If you see it as a stepping stone to your goal in pharmaceutical sales, it is. If you see it as a career barrier, it is.

Yet, very few of us have been taught to think of ourselves in terms of assets, as something that can be looked at in different ways, as something that can be developed and marketed to achieve the best we can be. Few have learned how to position themselves to stand for something that is in demand rather than something that is no longer in vogue. We don't know how to create positive perceptions in the minds of others about ourselves.

To get hired for your first job in pharmaceutical sales you'll need to start developing positive perceptions about yourself in the minds of people that can help you and with those that can actually hire you. You'll need to provide *mental links* that connect your skills and experience with what pharmaceutical sales managers are seeking in sales representatives. And show how your strengths are what's needed today. The exercise below will get you started.

Exercise: Look For Links With Your Past Experience

Directions:　Focus on your current job and your entire past career as you answer these questions.

What 5 things would you keep about your current job?

_____

_____

What 5 things would you eliminate?

_____

_____

What aspects of your career would you emphasize in defining yourself?

_____

_____

What would you downplay or eliminate?

_____

_____

What could you do tomorrow to get started?

Write it down in cursive. (It engages the brain)

Nor have many of us been taught that our jobs are something we can mold and shape and define. We can create projects and meaning to shape it in our own image. We can even create a career path into pharmaceutical sales by creating links with what we have done before in other jobs.

> ## Secret: Start Taking Charge Of Your Job Quest Now Or Take Orders For The Rest Of Your Life

There is work involved in a successful job quest in pharmaceutical sales. You'll need to do left brain work analyzing facts, trends and planning tactics. And you'll have to do right brain work where you'll need to tap into your intuition and creativity as you interpret learning, develop strategy, build relationships and make decisions.

The very first thing you need to do is to commit. You need to commit to taking charge of your job quest in pharmaceutical sales. Why do you desire this job? Are you willing to do what it takes? What's the best way to go about it? (We'll help you along with developing a game plan in the following chapters.) You need to answer questions about who you are, where you are now, and what you want to do with your life and career in this new area.

Of course, for many of us this is the sticky part. These are the very issues that we tend to avoid. Or, we make half efforts. Sometimes we live a life in which there is a conflict between who we are, what we want, and where we are heading. It's often helpful to look back at childhood career wishes and desires, to go back to an uncensored time, and look at what they reveal about your wants and what is holding you back.

In our workshops, we often find a disconnect between who people are, what they desire, and what they are doing. "I am doing 'X' now because I fell into it, but I really want to be doing 'Y' in the future." Or, "I'm not making the money I deserve, but I don't have the time to do anything about it." Or, "I've been wanting to explore a career in pharmaceutical sales, but I haven't done any-thing about it." Here's an exercise that will help you get started.

Exercise: What If?

Directions: Go to a quiet place where you can let your thoughts roam as you
answer these questions. Follow your instincts.

*What are you **really** passionate about? And what are you good at?*

_____

_____

What's your dream job? What would you do if you knew you couldn't fail?

_____

_____

Why does pharmaceutical sales appeal to you?

_____

_____

*What barriers are holding you back from getting your dream job in pharmaceutical
sales?*

_____

_____

Write it down in cursive. (Remember, it engages the brain.)

Our job fantasies reflect desires that we have put on hold in our lives. Many
people light up when we ask them to describe their dream job. It's, "Oh, if I
could live my dream, here's what I would be doing." And they go on to recount
something about pharmaceutical sales that has always intrigued them and
been at the back of their minds, but had never pursued or acted upon.

But as workplace philosophers like William Bridges and John Whyte point
out, desire is too powerful a motivator to leave untapped. We have all spent too
much time hiding who we are and doing what we are supposed to do, rather
than what we want to do. It's time to start living the dream you have for yourself in pharmaceutical sales. Now.

Secret: Breaking Up Is Hard To Do, But You Must

Many people have come to realize that there is no security in a job—*any* job. Today, we must be employable, not just employed.

Security lies in your ability to take charge. Security lies in your ability to see yourself as a brand and a one-person business. Security lies in your ability to respond to change and benefit from it, rather than hide from it. Security lies in your ability to develop a strategy and game plan to get from A to B to C. Security lies in you.

Even when you find your pharmaceutical sales job, it doesn't mean that you quit your quest. We can no longer count on a career at one company. That was your father's Oldsmobile. And, now Oldsmobile is gone too! We will not only work in multiple companies in our lifetimes, but most of us will have multiple careers.

Companies merge and split up. There are downsizings. The boss that hired you moves on. People are in trouble and need to point fingers. Technology and global economies have made "outsourcing" of jobs possible in ways never imagined just a few years ago. Even unimaginable terrorist activities are a possibility. Sales jobs are not immune. Managerial jobs are not immune.

With these kinds of changes the norm, you can't count on your company to keep you on the payroll. Companies focus on what's good for their bottom line, not your bottom line. Even when things are going well, they can quickly change. But if you have a personal branding mindset, you'll have options and a network in place. You'll be minding your own business, not just the company's business.

Exercise: Who's Looking Out For You?

Directions: Envision the following scenario. Imagine one day a major catastrophe occurs at your pharmaceutical company headquarters that breeds fear and uncertainty. A multi-billion dollar drug is abruptly pulled off the market, and sales in your company plummet. Then your boss walks into your office and says, "Sorry, I have some bad news for you. We have to downsize and your territory is being combined with Jim's." The job market is dreadful, particularly in the pharmaceutical industry and in your geographic area.

            What do you do now?

List the key people in your job network:

Core Business Network: *People you can really count on for introducing you around*

_____

_____

High Level Contacts: *Movers and Shakers who control decision making in their companies that you could call upon*

_____

_____

Weak Links: *Anyone you have ever met that you could call and achieve a level of recognition (and possible help)*

_____

_____

Write it down in cursive.

Secret: Write Down Your Thoughts And Ideas

     At the end of each exercise, we have asked you to write down your responses in cursive handwriting. Why is that? Writing down ideas and thoughts by hand in cursive script spurs the thought process. You actually come up with more ideas. You tend to probe things deeper. It fosters tapping into your right brain, into your creativity and intuition.

Write down what first comes to mind. Don't worry if it makes sense or not. No idea is a bad idea. Doodle with your ideas. Build one idea off another. Ruminate. Try not to filter your ideas. You can always transfer your ideas to your computer later and further revise and develop them.

> "I never know what I think about something until I read what I've written on it."
>
> —*William Faulkner*

Writing down answers to the exercises also indicates commitment. Maybe this time you'll do something about your stalled career. Or develop a game plan for landing your pharmaceutical sales job. In writing things down, you'll get ideas and inspiration that might not appear otherwise. It will help you finally start doing what you were meant to do with your life.

Writing in a journal or in this book will help you take charge of your job quest and think like a brand. After all, your goal is to prosper, not just survive. Like a brand manager in charge of any brand, you must change your strategy and tactics when the marketplace dynamics change. You look for new opportunities and needs that *your* brand can be the solution for.

Maybe the reason you picked up this book is that you have decided to stop conning yourself that you're doing something, when you are not doing much. Maybe it is time to get serious about pursuing a career in pharmaceutical sales.

—In A Nutshell—

Is there anything that people who have done great things with their careers have that you don't have?

Absolutely not.

Maybe it's time to take charge of your most important asset, *You.*

2.

Do Your Homework On The Pharmaceutical Industry

> "I find that the harder I work,
> the more luck I seem to have."
>
> —*Thomas Jefferson*

The best job in the industry is the sales representative job! It's fun. It pays well. You'll be working with intelligent, highly educated people: all the doctors and health care providers you call on every day. And, you'll be in a field that is important and dynamic, and sure to be around for a long time. A pharmaceutical sales job is also lots of work. But, if you like a professional, exciting working environment and can be flexible, this is the job for you.

In this chapter we want to give you a short primer on the pharmaceutical industry—the secrets of how the business really works—so that you'll be in the know. We'll even take you through the new rules and regulations as well as industry jargon so you'll know the ropes as you meet and interview with people in your job quest.

> ## Secret: It's A New Day In The Pharmaceutical Industry: Be Able To Talk About The Big Picture

Most people in the pharmaceutical business live, eat, and breathe the business. You'll need to know what is going on, too, if you want to impress people you meet on interviews.

The pharmaceutical industry has always been dynamic, but now the changes are revolutionary. New rules and regulations have eliminated traditional entertainment and other ways sales representatives sold to doctors. Doctors are busier than ever with more patients and more paperwork. No wonder they are frustrated.

On top of that, there is more competition in the pharmaceutical world than ever before. There are over 100,000 sales representatives tripping over each other trying to gain physician access. Yet, the pharmaceutical companies and sales representatives continue to do what worked in the past. It is not surprising because it was a model that worked for over fifty years.

The same old thing no longer works as well and physicians are responding. They are seeing fewer sales reps and listening less. The authors recently did a pilot study with MDs, NPs and PAs across the country that underscored this issue. In a nutshell, health care providers feel the relationship with sales reps is important, but only to the extent that the sales rep brings new information that is relevant to the practice.

Individual sales representatives are also having a difficult time breaking through all the noise of competitors. Reps are not differentiating themselves well. That's why we trademarked the slogan, "Schmoozing is out, science is in."™ To be successful today, a sales representative must provide *solutions* that will help physicians care for patients better. Rather than a traditional sales pitch, we believe sales calls should be more about the science behind a drug and how the drug can help physicians improve patient care.

Being aware of the changes taking place in the pharmaceutical industry will make you appear to be a player in the pharmaceutical industry, and that's what you want to be, after all. You can keep up to date on the trends in the business by checking into cafepharma.com or to trade magazines like *Pharmaceutical Executive, Pharma Voice, Pharma Marketing News,* and *Pharmaceutical Representative.*

Secret: Know The New Regulations In The PhRMA Code And How They Affect The Pharmaceutical Sales Rep

---

Part of a sales professional's job is building strong business relationships. Entertaining is one way relationships are built in business. Entertaining can range from expensive dinners to theater and sports events to bottles of wine. Entertaining is an acceptable practice in all industries with the exception of one—the pharmaceutical industry.

Why is that? The doctor-patient relationship is built on trust and confidence. A patient's trust must not be tampered with either intentionally, or in the perceptions of others. The public views prescribing the right treatment or drug as the responsibility of the doctor.

As patients, we all want to know that the drug being prescribed for us is the one that our healthcare provider believes to be the best choice for us based on scientific and clinical expertise, not because a doctor just had dinner with the sales representative. While there might be stories where healthcare providers changed their prescribing habits due to the dinner they had at a five-star restaurant, the author never had this experience in 14 years selling to doctors during a time when entertaining was allowed. Other representatives have also told us that they never had a healthcare provider start using a drug they were promoting or increase their prescribing of a drug because of their entertaining.

With the influx of sales representatives to the field and lack of time doctors have in their busy practices, entertaining in the '90s became the way of gaining access. At first, entertaining was acceptable. A sales representative got quality selling time with a doctor or a prescriber. And doctors were able to discuss a drug out of the office and without time away from patients. But eventually, entertaining became an issue for a variety of reasons—business, economic and political.

In July 2002, the Pharmaceutical Research and Manufacturers of America (PhRMA) created the voluntary PhRMA Code on Interactions with Healthcare Professionals. This code addresses interactions regarding marketed products and pre-launch activities for new drugs being introduced. Each pharmaceutical company was strongly encouraged to adopt in-house compliance polices.

The PhRMA Code Addresses:

- ❖ Basis of interactions between sales representatives and health care providers
- ❖ Informational presentations by or on behalf of a pharmaceutical company
- ❖ Third-party education or professional meetings
- ❖ Consultants to the industry
- ❖ Speaker training meetings
- ❖ Scholarship and education funds
- ❖ Educational and practice-related items
- ❖ Independence of decision making
- ❖ Adherence to the code

PhRMA Code Impact on Sales Reps:

❖ No entertaining of any kind.

❖ Spouses or guests are not permitted at education dinner meetings.

❖ All meals (whether lunch or dinner meetings) must be modest and must accompany a scientific or educational presentation.

❖ Items that are primarily for a patient's benefit may be given to prescribers, as long as they are not of substantial value (For example, a sales representative can give a prescriber a stethoscope.)

The PhRMA Code requires today's sales representative to sell a little differently and bring more value during the limited time they have with healthcare providers. (You can read the guidelines in their entirety at www.phrma.org)

Secret: Brush Up On HIPAA

Another new regulation you should know about is The Health Insurance Portability and Accountability Act of April 2003 (HIPAA). HIPAA is a voluminous document that covers many areas of patient privacy.

This regulation has had a dramatic effect on the lives of sales people. Many healthcare providers have chosen to close the door to sales people. Others have changed the where, how and if they will see representatives.

In a nutshell, under the HIPAA guidelines representatives cannot be in any area in a doctor's office where they may intentionally or accidentally hear or see patient information. For example, many offices have representatives wait to talk to the doctor in a lab or near a sample closet. These areas, as you know from your own doctor, are often in a hallway outside patient exam rooms. These are also areas where prescribers, nurses, and staff discuss patient cases, test results, and medications. So, you can see how this could be a problem if a representative is standing close by and overhearing these discussions.

Due to HIPAA, many offices have established very restrictive policies for sales representatives. Obviously, this makes selling very difficult for a sales representative. But, when you become a sales representative and you come across an office that refuses to see you for this reason, here's a suggestion you can make. Ask doctors if they would consider seeing you early before patients start coming, or at the end of the day after all patients have been seen. You could even ask if you could wait in the prescriber's office. All they can do is say, "No."

But, as the saying goes, "nothing ventured, nothing gained." By doing this, you demonstrate your respect for their office policy and your need to share some very important information in a way that fits with their office procedures.

Secret: Know About The OIG Guidance For Pharmaceutical Companies

---

The OIG (Office Of Inspector General) has weighed in with their own compliance program guidance. The OIG's final document warns that providing doctors with gifts, recreation, travel, meals, and entertainment could violate fraud, abuse, and anti-kickback laws. OIG encourages companies to adopt voluntary internal compliance policies that promote adherence to acceptable practices. As a result, companies have devoted considerable time and resources to foster cultures that prevent and detect these sorts of problems. You can read about the OIG guidance in its entirety at http://oig.hhs.gov.

OIG Recommendations for Pharma Companies:

- Implementing written policies and procedures
- Designating a compliance officer
- Conducting effective training and education for all employees
- Conducting internal monitoring and auditing
- Enforcing standards through disciplinary actions
- Responding to problems and implementing corrections

OIG Regulations Impact on Sales Reps:

- Meetings with prescribers are small and less lavish.
- Meeting location is under scrutiny because certain destinations are viewed as vacation spots not conducive to education.
- Hotels with the words "spa" or "resort" are considered suspect of excess.
- Events are limited to healthcare providers only with no guests.
- No gifts, entertainment, or recreation can be provided.
- Any hint of impropriety or excess should be avoided.

Secret: Learn The Lingo Of The Pharmaceutical Industry

Every industry has its own lingo but the pharmaceutical industry may have set the record in terms of its own code words and shorthand. But, you have to learn "Pharma speak" if you want to fit in on interviews and join the team.

Key Pharma Buzzwords:

The Field And Its Lingo

The Field:	Field representatives, field sales, district managers, managed care area managers. The field is a term used for all employees who work outside the home office.
Rep:	All pharmaceutical sales representatives are commonly called "reps."
Primary Care Rep:	Sales rep selling to prescribers office-to-office, pharmacies and, sometimes, very small hospitals in the local community. Sales are directed to internists, family practitioners, pediatricians, nurse practitioners and physician assistants. Primary care sales reps also cover some specialists.
Specialty Rep:	Sales rep who calls on specialists, such as cardiologists, gastroenterologists and oncologists. Specialty sales is a promotion from primary care sales.
Hospital Rep:	Sales representative who calls on large hospitals (over 300 beds) and teaching hospitals.
DM:	District Manager assigned to manage 12–18 representatives who make up a district.
Territory:	The area a representative works that is defined by zipcodes. Representatives are assigned a specific list of prescribers to call on. They do not go outside their territory to call on their prescribers unless invited by another rep.

The Field And Its Lingo, *continued*

Cluster/Pod: 4–5 representatives assigned to work the same territory. Most, if not all, territory activities are coordinated with your team members.

District: A district is made up of around 12–15 territories. So, each DM would supervise 12–15 reps. For example, the Mid Atlantic District might cover Delaware, Maryland, Washington DC and Virginia.

Prescriber: Health care professional who can prescribe medication to patients. This is your target audience: physicians, nurse practitioners and physician assistants.

Doc: My "docs". Reps often refer to a physician as "one of my docs said."

NP: Nurse practitioner. NPs treat patients and prescribe medication under their own signature.

PA: Physician assistant. PAs treat patients and prescribe medication under the supervision of an MD.

Prescription: The written order of a physician or other licensed practitioner (for example, a NP or PA) that directs a pharmacist to dispense a medication.

Script: An abbreviation for "prescription."

The Bag: The briefcase used to carry samples. Most companies issue a bag, but reps soon find other totes and carriers with wheels that are more comfortable to use during the day. Also used figuratively: "I carried the bag for 15 years." Carrying the bag refers to being a field sales rep.

Product Mix: The different products you are assigned to promote.

Product Line Up: The order your products are sold in. The products you sell first, second, and third are determined by corporate objectives.

The Field And Its Lingo, *continued*

Ride Along: Any guest spending the day with a representative in their territory making calls. The word "ride along" refers both to the guest and the activity.

Field Evaluation: This is a follow-up report that a DM writes after each ride along with a sales representative.

Detail Piece: A pharmaceutical sales piece on a specific drug with the marketing message based on efficacy and safety.

Detailing: Selling and detailing are interchangeable. For example, a rep speaks of "detailing" doctors, not "selling."

PI: Package insert. A paper with the prescribing drug information approved by the FDA found in every sample box. Reps often use the PI when a doctor asks a specific question about a side effect or other issue. Doctors often ask specifically, "What does your PI say?"

Samples: Trial size of the product or drug left for prescribers to give to patients for trial along with their prescription.

Laptop Letters: Promotional letters that reps send out to prescribers via their laptop. Laptop letters have been written by the marketing department and approved for use by the pharmaceutical company's legal department.

Presentation Binder: The binder reps carry that holds detail pieces, clinical papers, package inserts and other information used for detailing.

Placebo Demonstrators: Sometimes drugs such as an inhaler for asthma have demos—an inhaler with no drug—which reps give to nurses to use as a teaching tool.

Promotional Literature: All marketing materials approved by the company's legal department for use in detailing.

OTC: Non-prescription medications that can be purchased over-the-counter.

On Label Promotion: The selling of a product for its approved use.

The Field And Its Lingo, *continued*

Off Label Promotion: The selling of a product for unapproved uses. This is prohibited by the FDA. Therefore, there is zero tolerance by companies for sales reps selling a product for unapproved uses.

DIS Letter: Letter from the Drug Information Services (DIS) department in your company that responds to a prescriber question or special request.

Indication: The use for which a drug is approved.

"Gold Standard" Drug: This term refers to drugs that have been on the market for a long time and have proven themselves to be very effective and safe. Gold standard drugs are the drugs to which all others in their class are compared.

Home Office: Corporate headquarters.

Home Office Guest: A VP, Product Manager, Sales Trainer, or other employee from corporate headquarters who accompanies the rep in the field for a ride along. The term "ride along" is more common today.

RD or RM: Regional Director. Also called a Regional Manager or RM. RDs are in charge of DMs. The country is divided into regions—East, West, Mid West, South. While RDs often work out of their homes, they are considered home office personnel.

Product Manager: Individual charged with stewarding a particular product toward increased market share, determining the marketing message and propelling future growth.

Sales Training: Training is ongoing throughout a pharmaceutical sales career. Initial training includes product knowledge, company and industry introductions, and basic selling the company/industry way. Training takes place in a variety of venues: in person, at the Home Office, at national and regional meetings, online and in the territory.

Guidelines and Regulations

PhRMA Guidelines: The guidelines developed by PhRMA—Pharmaceutical Research and Manufacturers of America, the industry's trade association. The guidelines set out the acceptable interactions between sales representatives and prescribers.

HIPAA: Health Insurance Portability and Accountability Act of April 2003. This privacy rule protects patient information. As a result, many prescribers have changed where and how they will see sales representatives.

OIG: Office Of Inspector General. The OIG guidelines indicate that providing doctors with gifts, recreation, travel, meals, and entertainment could violate fraud, abuse, and anti-kickback laws. OIG encourages companies to adopt voluntary internal compliance policies that promote adherence to acceptable practices.

Professional Education

CME: Continuing Medical Education. This is required, ongoing accredited education for MDs.

CE: Continuing Education. This is required, ongoing accredited education for nurses, pharmacists, physician assistants and nurse practitioners.

Marketing

Promotional literature: All marketing materials must be approved by a company's legal department for use in detailing.

DTC: Direct-to-consumer advertising. These are the TV and radio ads promoting a drug that reach a broad audience.

DTP: Direct-to-patient advertising. DTP advertising is internet marketing where patients with a specific disease can seek out information proactively on the company's website.

Managed Care

MCO: Managed care organizations.

Managed Markets: Each company has its own name for reps who call on managed care organizations. These reps negotiate formulary status, price and other issues. These professionals typically started their career as sales reps, may have worked in marketing and sales training, and were District Managers.

Formulary: A list of drugs approved for use by managed care. Prescribers must adhere to using drugs on the list of each MCO.

PDL: Preferred Drug List. A list of drugs on managed care lists that have earned some preferred status due to efficacy, safety or cost.

Sources of Clinical Information

Journal Articles: This term refers to articles published in journals such as *The New England Journal of Medicine.*

Studies: Research being done on new drugs or drugs requesting approval for another indication (use for another disease).

Investigator: Physicians participating in studies are referred to as investigators.

Clinical Paper: Investigators write the results of a study. This paper is very thorough and covers everything from the number of participating human subjects, the methodology, drugs and placebos used, adverse events, efficacy and outcomes.

Food and Drug Administration (FDA)

The FDA has the responsibility of reviewing the massive research data presented by pharmaceutical companies seeking approval for a new drug or approval of a new indication for a drug already on the market. The FDA is the governmental agency responsible for approving all marketed drugs in the U.S.

Once a drug is approved, the FDA has the responsibility of continuously monitoring the efficacy and safety of drugs. This agency also oversees the marketing and promotional activity of each drug so that unsubstantiated claims and biased information are not given to the public. The FDA approves the color of the pill (or device), the name, the box or container that contains the drug. Everything about the product requires approval.

New Drug Process

This is an abbreviated version. The complete process can be found on the web at FDA.gov.

❖ **Pre-clinical Trials:** Animal tests determine chemical, biological, and pharmaceutical properties. Trials look for toxicity levels, such as a lethal dose, effective dose and the margin of safety. They determine a drug's effect on the heart, liver, kidneys and other organs and tissues. In short, pre-clinical trials look at pharmacokinetics—how the drug is absorbed, distributed, metabolized and excreted.

❖ **Investigational New Drug Application:** IND. A company submits results of pre-clinical trials and product information to the FDA requesting approval for clinical trials. The IND contains all the information about a compound.

❖ **Clinical Trials:** Clinical trials are prospective research investigations conducted in human subjects to answer specific questions about a drug.

■ **Phase I Trials:** Phase I establishes safe dosage ranges for experimental drugs on a small number of subjects, usually less than 100 healthy people.

■ **Phase II Trials:** Phase II tests the experimental drug's effectiveness in treating the disease for which it is developed. Approximately 100–200 people who suffer with the targeted disease are used in these tests.

■ **Phase III Trials:** Phase III can take two or more years. The drug is given to hundreds or thousands of consenting people who are diagnosed with the disease the drug is intended to treat. These clinical trials are conducted to establish the efficacy and safety of the drug, and to identify any possibly serious side effects that haven't occurred in the early trials.

❖ **NDA:** New Drug Application. Upon completion of the clinical trials, if the results demonstrate evidence of the drug effectiveness and safety under the exact conditions of use in the proposed labeling (PI), a company may submit an NDA to the FDA. The NDA includes a huge amount of data from all phases of the drug development process.

A Drug Has Three Names

❖ **Chemical Name:** A drug's chemical name is based on its structure and conforms to a set of international rules.

❖ **Generic Name:** This is its common name, often a version of the chemical name. The generic name is used when referring to the drug in literature. Drugs with the same chemical structure share the same generic name. For example, acetaminophen is a generic name.

❖ **Trade or Brand Name:** Identifies a drug as a product of a specific company. For example, Tylenol is the brand name; the company is McNeil.

Licensing of Drugs

Patent: License to produce and market a drug exclusively. After a patent expires, other companies may also produce and market the product, under either a generic name or a different brand name.

Patent Life: 17 years. It usually takes 10–12 years to bring a drug to market, so a company only has approximately five years to recoup an investment and make a profit.

As you can see, this world is full of buzzwords and has its own way of talking about the industry and the job of the sales representative. Knowing the jargon and being able to use it in your meetings and interviews will help you be perceived as part of the pharmaceutical world.

Secret: Know The Basics About The Day-To-Day Job Of A Pharmaceutical Sales Representative

---

A typical day for a sales representative starts around 8 a.m. checking voice mail. Voice mail is the life blood of day-to-day activity of a pharmaceutical sales rep. This is where you keep in touch with colleagues, your manager and the home office. Sometimes, your customers will leave messages for you as well. After responding to voicemails, you need to check your samples in your car trunk to make sure you have enough for the day. (Some reps pack their cars at night to keep things running smoothly.)

Now, you are ready to go out for the day.

So, where do you go?

Effective sales representatives have their territory mapped out in a four-to six-week cycle. You map out your territory and coordinate your plans with the other representatives in your cluster, the four to five other sales reps from your company that have the same territory.

You make your appointments based on this map and drop-in calls fit in around appointments and best times to see prescribers. (Prescribers are the MDs and other healthcare providers who can write prescriptions. See buzz-word section of the chapter). On average, a sales representative makes ten to twelve calls a day depending on the territory. Usually, this can be accomplished with good planning.

Once you arrive in the parking lot at the first office, you should review your notes from the previous call to develop your strategy before you go in. As a sales rep, your main goal is to persuade the prescriber to increase writing prescriptions of your drug or, at the very least, to move toward that end. Be prepared and plan your strategy before each call you make. Getting in front of a prescriber with no pre-call plan is unproductive and a waste of time for both you and the prescriber.

Doctors are very busy. Once you are in front of the prescriber, your time will be limited, so you need to communicate your message clearly and succinctly. With time so limited, you need to work with all the staff in the office to uncover needs and opportunities. This strategy will allow you to sell more effectively. The staff includes the receptionist, the nurse, the office manager, the lab technician, and anyone else who can give you a deeper insight into the practice. You need to learn what the challenges of the day-to-day practice are, and to provide your drug and your company's resources as the solution. Before leaving the office, you can schedule another appointment if needed, and check the sample closet and leave more samples.

You should always leave the office knowing more than you knew prior to the call. Pharmaceutical sales is based on the building blocks of uncovering needs and opportunities, providing solutions and building business relationships that will earn continued and increased business.

When you return to your car, you should write your post call notes. Most likely, you came out with some new information that you need to follow up on when you make your next call. Or, it may be a request for information that can only be sent from the home office. Your notes should include all the information that your company requires. If you do the call notes right away you won't need to jog your memory later. And, you'll be prepared when you make your next visit to the doctor's office.

Sometimes the request might be for samples that you didn't have because your inventory was depleted and you were waiting for your monthly delivery. When that happens, you can leave a voicemail message with another rep in your cluster to drop samples off the next time they are calling on the office. Then, you're off to the next call to do it all over again!

There are times when you will not be able to talk to a prescriber, but the office will need samples, so a staff member will get you a signature. Since you took the time and energy to get out of the car, pack your bag and walk from the parking lot into the office, at least work the staff! The staff will tell you a lot and will be pleased that you chose to talk business with them.

Be different than the other sales reps. Many reps view medical office staff as just people with whom to have a quick chat. While some of that is fine and necessary to building relationships, at least strive to learn something about the prescriber and the practice that you didn't know when you arrived. The staff will even tell you things about other representatives and this is good intelligence. Maybe the representative selling your competing product goes home at noon. That's an edge you ought to know about.

Primary care offices typically close from 12 to 2 pm. This is when the doctor makes hospital rounds. What does a rep do during this down time?

If you don't have a lunch appointment, you make pharmacy calls. There are independent pharmacies (like the ones in the lobby of a medical building) as well as chain pharmacies (like in your grocery store) you should consider calling on. You should "detail" or sell to the pharmacist as you would any prescriber. Inquire about patient needs and ask questions. Leave patient educational literature and gather any other type of information the pharmacist might know and be willing to share. For example, maybe the pharmacist knows about a new prescriber coming to your territory, or, maybe one of your competitors has left the area. All of this is good business intelligence.

Now, you've done this ten or twelve times and it's time to head home. The day is over. Well, not quite. You have to go home and finish making phone calls if you haven't completed all of them while in the field. You need to communicate all your calls and the sample activity of the day to your home office via your laptop. Of course, you need to check and respond to email and voicemail. Perhaps you have a new project that is due tomorrow morning. (Yes, this happens). You might have some on-line tests to take and you certainly have to prepare for your day tomorrow.

> ## Secret: Know How A Rep Is Evaluated So That You Can Emphasize Similar Strengths In Your Skill Set

Typically, a sales representative works independently as you can see from the day-in-the-life scenario we sketched out in the last Secret.

So how are you developed and coached? How are you evaluated? Good question. You get a *ride along* with your manager several times a quarter. Together with your sales numbers, the ride along with your manager is an important way the company assesses how you are progressing in the field. This also gives the manager an opportunity to provide coaching and on-going training.

What is the ride along like? It depends on the manager. A manager can make or break the job. We've heard stories ranging from managers who don't speak a word all day, to taskmasters who criticize all day to managers who are true partners and help uncover new business opportunities in your territory.

At the end of this day, you and your manager will sit in the car or have a cup of coffee in a restaurant while you discuss the events that occurred during the day. Then, the manager writes a field evaluation report. The report shows what you did well and what skills need improvement.

Key Areas Rated on the Field Evaluation Report:

Territory Analysis Planning:

- ❖ Know your business: Who are your top 15–20 prescribers?
- ❖ Know where you are going: Your territory should be mapped out 4–6 weeks in advance.
- ❖ Identify your opportunities: Perhaps a thought leader wants to speak at a community hospital that would impact your territory.

Business Development

- ❖ Know what resources are available to you, such as slides or patient education materials.
- ❖ Let your customers know that you have knowledge and access to company resources that you don't carry in your bag.
- ❖ Know something about the work habits of the reps you compete with—this is valuable intelligence.

❖ Know what is going on at community hospitals in their patient education departments.

❖ Have a pre-call plan.

❖ Uncover the winnable position and sell your drug against competitive drugs with each prescriber.

❖ Know your customer's day-to-day challenges and create appropriate solutions.

Account Development

❖ Know your customer needs and how to meet them.

❖ Uncover the best way to position and sell your drug against competitive drugs with each prescriber.

Technical Knowledge

❖ Be the expert on all the drugs you sell and on your competitors' drugs.

❖ Be well read. Stay current with journals, clinical papers and the lay press.

Selling Skills

❖ Sell effectively and creatively.

❖ Uncover a customer's winnable position.

❖ Be customer-focused.

Administration

❖ Stay on top of paperwork, voicemail, email, bi-monthly expense reports, activity reports and other correspondence.

Teamwork

❖ Be a team player with colleagues calling on the same prescribers. Share ideas and information.

❖ Share best practices.

❖ Be a part of the solution, not the problem.

Urgency

❖ Be responsive. This industry works in a constant state of urgency.

Accountability

❖ Work within company policies, adhering to all regulations and guidelines. Ethical behavior is expected at all times.

❖ Be accountable for increasing market share.

Sales Representative Rating System:

O	Outstanding	exceptional performance
V	Very Good	above average performance, proficiency requirements exceeded
G	Good	average performance, meets standards
I	Improvement needed	proficiency deficient
U	Unsatisfactory	results generally unacceptable
N	Not rated	could be new to job

You do need to pay attention to your manager's field report because the next time your manager rides with you, it will come up again. The manager will say something like, "Last time we worked together, we discussed working on a stronger close. I didn't see improvement in that area today."

So, pay attention and keep copies of the report. You'll also want to use good reports when applying for future positions.

As a person breaking into pharmaceutical sales, pay attention to what is called for to do the job well. Link your own experiences and strengths to what is needed in the job, so that people can tangibly see how you could be successful as a pharmaceutical sales representative. Here is an exercise to get you started.

Exercise: Linking Your Background To The Sales Rep Job

Directions: Look for similarities in the strengths and skills you have with the job of a pharmaceutical sales representative.

Business Knowledge: *Demonstrate how you learned a complicated business from a prior job:*

_____

_____

Advance Planning: *Show how you planned sales or other business activities in your jobs:*

_____

_____

Identifying Opportunities: *List new ideas or programs you introduced in the past:*

_____

_____

Business Development: *Show innovative things you did to increase business or sales:*

_____

_____

Account Development: *Demonstrate how you responded to customer needs that resulted in increased business, or how you positioned your product successfully against a competitor's product.*

_____

_____

Technical Knowledge: *Show how you were very knowledgeable in a technical area:*

_____

_____

Selling Skills: *Indicate things you've done that show how you sell effectively.*

Administration: *Cite past experience that demonstrates good organization and responsiveness to voicemail and email:*

Teamwork: *List joint projects and activities that demonstrate teamwork*

Urgency: *Demonstrate job responsiveness:*

Accountability: *Show how you adhere to all company guidelines:*

Write it down in cursive.

—In A Nutshell—

You'll do a lot better in your job quest if you learn how to talk the talk.
Learn the basics about how the industry works.
Link your experiences to the job of the rep.

3.

Have A Strategy For Building Inroads Into The Pharmaceutical Industry

"Would you tell me, please, which way I ought to go from
here?" asked Alice.
"That depends a good deal on where you want to go,"
said the Cat.
"I don't much care where,"
said Alice.
"Then it doesn't matter which way you go,"
said the Cat.

—*Lewis Carroll's* "Alice in Wonderland"

How can you penetrate the pharmaceutical industry? How can you find out about jobs? What avenues make the most sense? What's a waste of your time? How can you get closer to the hiring manager? How can you get the job? If you're like most people, these are some of the questions you need to find answers to.

Unfortunately, there is no yellow brick road to take you there. There is no one right path. But, some roads will be more effective for you than others. In this chapter, we'll be talking about how to develop a smart search game plan.

Networking is the underpinning of that game plan. "Well, you're probably thinking, how can I build a network in the pharmaceutical industry? I don't know anyone there. I never worked there." But you can do it. And you, no doubt, know people who can help you. Here's the first step.

Secret: You Already Know People Who Can Help You

You already have contacts at your fingertips: your own physician, a nurse, specialists that you see, your child's pediatrician, receptionists and your pharmacist. Any of these people would likely be very willing to give you the names and contact information of some of the sales representatives that call on them.

Most doctors and nurses have dozens of sales reps calling on them every week. These sales representatives all work for pharmaceutical companies that could have a job that is just right for you. That's exactly how a number of our rep friends got their start in pharmaceutical sales. And there is no reason it can't work for you, too.

Explain to your doctor (or nurse, or other healthcare provider) that you want to break into pharmaceutical sales. Tell them you want to talk to some sales reps to find out more about the business. Be sure to emphasize that you're not looking for someone to give you a job. You just want to talk to people in the field to learn more about it as a career for you.

If you see someone carrying a briefcase around a medical complex and think it might be a sales rep, stop them and ask questions. Many sales reps we know have been stopped like this many times throughout their careers.

Most representatives are friendly enough that they will give you some information or their card, and even invite you to call them. Throughout fourteen years in the field, the author was asked by many physicians and nurses to talk to their patients, family members or friends who wanted to learn about becoming a sales representative. Your doctor will likely do the same. (If not, maybe you need to find a new doctor!)

Don't worry about your doctor's sales rep not wanting to talk to you. If your doctor's sales representatives are like most, you will always get a return phone call. Sales representatives enjoy talking about the job and the industry. Pharmaceutical sales reps are very friendly people and are willing to help. (That's just one of the reasons you are going to like this field.)

Besides, your doctor is an important client of the sales representative. Chances are they will try to help you so that you'll have good things to report back. Here's a handy exercise to develop your doctor referral list.

Exercise: Building The Doc Network

Directions: Write down all the medical professionals you could ask to put you in touch with some pharmaceutical sales representatives so that you can learn more about the business. These can be your primary care doctor or specialists you see. Include doctors that your spouse or children see.

_____

_____

_____

_____

_____

> ## Secret: Focus Initially On Building Relationships, Not On Finding A Job

Think of this as a contact sport and a numbers game. Don't rely on just one contact. You've got to really work the system. When you get one name, ask for another name. Eventually, you'll get to where you want to be—impressing the hiring manager and landing the job!

At this early stage, your goal is to build a broad network of contacts in the industry. You can expand your list beyond your doctors to include anyone else you might know who works in a hospital or for a pharmaceutical company.

Don't say right off the bat that you don't know anyone. You may not. But if you take a networking approach, and start telling people what your goal is, the people you tell might know people in the industry. When you do talk to people, ask them questions about the industry. Ask them how they got into the industry. Get them talking. Don't try to sell yourself right away. Above all, don't talk about a job right away unless you are responding to an ad for a specific position.

In each meeting, your goal is to connect with them personally, and to start to build a relationship. Of course, you can weave in some of the skills and strengths that are similar to the representative job that you outlined in chapter two. What you want to do is build a personal relationship with the person, and leave them with mental links between what you have done and why you can be a success in pharmaceutical sales.

As you meet with each person, your goal is to get two more names. Toward the end of the interview, you can ask something like, "Is there anyone else I should talk to as I explore the industry?"

Secret: Don't Drop The Ball After The First Meeting

Most people drop the ball after the initial interview.

Don't. Stay in touch.

You would be surprised how things can change, and an opportunity might spring up later. And if you are still top of mind, you'll get referred. After each interview, write the person a short note thanking them for their time and any other contacts they gave you. Keep in touch later by email. Let them know who else you are meeting with and how your job quest is going. You can ask for advice on a particular issue, or ask a specific question about a new company that you will be meeting with.

If you're taking the networking approach we are describing, in not too long a time, you will have an army of people in the pharmaceutical industry you can turn to for insight and advice. Remember, most job seekers drop the ball after the initial interview and follow-up letter. It's short-sighted.

And don't drop the ball after you get the job, either. You can always put them on your holiday card list, or send an article you think they might find of interest. You'll want your network in place when you look for a promotion down the road.

Remember, if you build relationships broadly in the pharmaceutical industry, you won't ever be left up the creek. You'll always be able to paddle your way out—just call on your network. Here is an exercise to get you started in network building.

Exercise: Expanding Your Network

Directions: Now, write down the names of people you know who work in hospitals or for pharmaceutical companies in any capacity that might be able to help you.

_____

_____

_____

_____

Develop another list of people who you know that might know people who work in hospitals or the pharmaceutical industry.

_____

_____

_____

_____

Start calling the people on your lists to tell them about your job quest and ask them if they know people you can talk to in the field for an informational interview.

Start now. One group that can help a lot are sales representatives.

Secret: Sales Reps Are Great Contacts Because They Make Money If They Refer A Successful Candidate

---

You might be wondering, "Why should I waste my time meeting with pharmaceutical sales reps? A sales rep has the job I want. They can't hire me."

True, a sales representative can't hire you. Their manager can, though.

But, there is something in it for the rep—a finder's fee if they refer you to a hiring manager and you get the job. So, sales representatives have a financial incentive to refer you if they feel that you could be a good sales rep at their company.

That's why if you connect well with the sales representative your doctor or someone else introduced you to on the phone, the rep will offer to forward your resume to their manager. This is great news. If a sales representative offers to forward your resume to a manager, it is because the rep sees something in you that is a fit. The rep will look good in the eyes of their boss, the hiring manager. And, if you are hired, the representative receives a finder's fee as we told you. This makes for a great story to tell a manager when you finally get a job in the industry.

Secret: Develop A Focus List Of Your Key Prospects

You want to be as strategic as possible in your job search. You don't have time to go after every company out there. We have always found that it is smart to build a focus list of prospects. This is your core list. Sending out a mass mailing to hundreds of pharmaceutical companies is not the best way to spend your time. Be strategic and focus your efforts where you can get the most results.

Most important on the focus list are companies where you have an internal contact. That's why networking is crucial. Your resume and application will always get extra attention if you are associated with someone on the inside. This is true even if that inside person is someone you just met, but you hit it off with. Having an internal contact gives you a tremendous advantage, particularly if there are other candidates with similar qualifications. And, you now have an internal name to use in letters and in interviews. You are on your way to being a member of the team.

Another hot group on your focus list would be companies that are hiring, companies that have real live openings for sales reps. You can find these out through company web sites, recruiters, job fairs, newspaper ads and word of mouth.

The third area that holds promise is a company that has products in an area of interest to you, where there is a connection to your background. You are looking for companies where your "story"—your background and interests—link well to the job. For example, many people with sales experience in other areas get into the industry because of a family member who has a particular disease. Sometimes, a nurse or others in the healthcare field have used this strategy successfully for breaking into the business. For example, if you are a nurse who knows a lot about a certain specialty or has an interest in a particular class of therapies, you can focus on the leading companies in that area.

We also think it is important to add to the focus list a short wish list—your Top Ten List—where you'd love to work either because of the company's reputation, values, product line, culture or the top-flight training you would receive. These could be the most well known pharmaceutical brands, or it could be a smaller company that you heard is a really terrific, people-oriented place to work. This is your dream list. And, of course, the bigger your network gets, the better your chances for landing there.

In short, what you are looking for is a smart strategy for you. Here's an exercise to help you organize your list of focus companies.

Exercise: Developing A Focus List

Directions: Write down the key companies in each category so that you can prioritize your job hunt.

Companies where you have contacts. *Any company where you have developed a relationship through your doctor or colleagues should be on your core list. You will always get more attention.*

Companies with job openings. *Fish where the fish are. Companies advertising for a sales representative to cover a territory are hot prospects. They have a need for someone like you. Check out job fairs, recruiters, company web sites and local classified ads.*

Companies with leadership in an area of interest to you. *If you have an interest in a particular area of medicine, you can focus in on companies that have a leading drug in this area.*

Top pharmaceutical companies. *It's always good to work for a leading company since you will get great training and other benefits, and it will always be a credential to market yourself with in the future.*

> ## Secret: Networking Is The Number One Way Most People Get Into Pharmaceutical Sales

---

That's why the best thing to do is ask your MDs, pharmacists, or friends if they know anyone who works in the industry who would be willing to talk to you. Most of the representatives we know have said, "It was really just who I knew. It's very hard to get into this industry." Or, "It's really all about making connections." Very rarely do we hear stories of a rep who blindly submitted a resume to a company or DM without someone advocating for that the person to at least get an interview.

But, the interesting thing is, your internal contact does not have to be someone you know very well. Often it is the "weak link," someone you just met who you hit it off with or a friend of a friend that will help you the most in your quest.

This is a numbers game. If you are truly interested, you have to keep up the hunt and not get discouraged because you are initially rejected. And you shouldn't limit your networking to people in the medical profession or just one contact. Opportunity can come from anywhere. Here's the story of a sales rep who got his breakthrough networking on a golf course.

Troy's Story

I began my sales career at Dun & Bradstreet selling financial services. Then, I got a job with the Yellow Pages selling space to dentists, doctors, and chiropractors. After six years of selling experience and so much of that time spent with physicians, a logical next step seemed to be pharmaceutical sales. As luck would have it, I was playing golf one day and met a pharmaceutical sales representative on the course. This rep gave me an inside look at what life was like in the world of pharmaceutical sales. He recommended a recruiter who I immediately called and set up an interview.

I interviewed with three different pharmaceutical companies. The most memorable was with one of the top five pharmaceutical companies. It was a day-long series where I went through five interviews. The fifth interview was in front of a panel of five people. The panel included two district managers, two HR people and one person that may have been a trainer.

At a different pharmaceutical company interview I was asked to sell the yellow pages to the hiring manager. Then, they handed me a pen, and asked me to sell the pen. Other questions asked were:

- ❖ *What is your day like?*
- ❖ *What do you know about this company?*
- ❖ *What are your strengths? Your weaknesses?*
- ❖ *How do you handle conflict? ('By the way,' the interviewer added, 'the correct answer to this is "very well". So what I really want is for you to follow-up with a story that demonstrates your answer to be true. This is very important because conflict handling and team selling are key to successful sales.')*

I thought this interview went well and wanted the job. So what happened next totally surprised me. I called the hiring manager to follow up, but the manager did not return the calls. After several attempts, I wrote a note (this was before email) and faxed it to the manager. Later, the manager told me that he intentionally did not return the phone calls because he wanted to see what I would do. He wanted to see if I would be persistent. I was. So, I got the job.

Joan's Story

I was living in Atlanta, Georgia, and had been teaching school for three years but wanted to explore other opportunities. As luck would have it, I met a former physical educational teacher at a party who was now a hospital sales rep. I was very intrigued about his job and he told me that the industry was looking to bring more women into sales and he invited me to a hospital conference with ten pharmaceutical companies. Taking him up on his offer was the best thing I ever did. I talked to every rep there, asked questions about their company, and decided then and there that this is what I wanted to do

Within two weeks, I received a phone call from one, and was invited to fly to Chicago to interview. As a former teacher, I was so excited to fly to Chicago on business, and was excited to have the interview with the VP of Sales. As it turned out, they did indeed call about three months after the interview to offer me a sales position in Ohio. By then I had made the personal decision to move back to Florida, where I had attended school at the University of Miami.

While in Miami, I began interviewing with several pharmaceutical companies. Nothing came of it. At this time, I thought to myself, "How could I have not taken that position in Ohio?" But I knew that you have to live where you want to live as well. Finally, I did obtain a sales position with a dental company. I was in heaven! I loved sales, my clients, and the territory.

Well, as I went along in life, I met a wonderful man and moved to Minnesota. I still wanted to get on board with a pharmaceutical company, so I contacted several recruiters and the interviews just came out of the woodwork now that I had sales experience. I went to work for one, and from that point on I never looked back.

All in all I have spent eight years as a pharmaceutical sales representative (moving back to Florida and then to Texas as my family moved), one year in the home office as a Sales Training Manager, and the last 14 years as a District Manager in both the Chicago and in the Baltimore—Washington, DC market. My career path has been a very classic one—working my way up the ladder to being a Senior District Manager. I am still energized by the will to win in each and every sales call.

Meg's Story

I had been selling engineering products for three years and had a very successful track record. One year, I was #1 in the nation. Another year I was #2 in the nation. I was expecting my second child and wanted something that had flexible hours. I was familiar with pharmaceutical sales because my father-in-law is a physician. I had no idea if the pharmaceutical industry offered flextime positions or how to even get started in trying to find out. Naturally, I turned to my father-in-law who gave me the business cards of several representatives who called on him. I contacted each one to learn more about the job.

By chance, I happened to read the classified ads one Sunday and saw an ad for a flextime position. I was interviewed and after the fourth interview, I was offered the job. The manager wanted me to start in April, but due to my pregnancy I was not available to start until October. The manager was so impressed with my sales record that she held the job for me.

Ten years later, I was ready to move into specialty sales. I started my job hunt by doing a web search on www.cafepharma.com. I went through the list of all companies that had a link to its career sites and submitted my resume. I checked the website every night and sent out more resumes.

My search was very focused because I had disease states in mind that I wanted to sell, and concentrated on the companies that had products in these markets. Some of the companies linked to recruiters, others received the resume directly. My focus paid off. Within less than a year and numerous interviews, I got the specialty job of my dreams.

Secret: If You Have Sales Experience, Recruiters Can Help You

Recruiters are another avenue many people use to break into pharmaceutical sales. Recruiters typically have contracts with a specific district manager. Sometimes, a recruiter works for a company division, such as the allergy division. If a company is working with a specific recruiting firm, the company will usually post it somewhere on the career site. If you find the recruiter's company name on the job site, call that company and ask for the recruiter who is working for J&J or whatever company you're interested in.

The first question a recruiter will ask is "Do you have sales experience?" If the answer is yes, they'll ask you to send your resume. If your answer is no, they'll tell you to go get some and call them in two to three years.

You can find recruiters online when you search on the internet for "pharmaceutical sales recruiters." But most often, you'll come into contact with recruiters through networking. Most reps probably keep in touch with two to three recruiters as they frequently get called themselves.

Just like any industry, recruiters are a good source of what's going on at the various firms, who is hiring and who is cutting back. If the sales rep that a recruiter calls isn't interested in a job, smart reps refer other people so the rep will stay in the loop and be top of mind with the recruiter. It's a good way to build a relationship with a recruiter, and get calls in the future about jobs that may be right for you.

Reps always share job information they get from recruiters with each other. Recruiters also get the names of representatives from doctor's offices as well as other representatives, so the strength of your network will always come into play.

Steve's Story

I had been a nurse for about ten years when I decided that I wanted to get a job with a business orientation. As a nurse, of course, I was aware of pharmaceutical and medical sales but I didn't know how to approach the business. So I contacted a recruiter who placed me with a surgical supply company. Then, I went into IV home care. But I wanted eventually to get into pharmaceutical sales. A while later, I heard that one of my former supervisors was working at a pharmaceutical company, and I called him and an interview was set up.

At the interview, I was given a clinical paper to present. I had no idea how to present anything, least of all a clinical paper. I didn't even understand any of the language.

But, I had an idea. During the time I was given to prepare for the presentation, I color-coded the different sections of the clinical paper. For example, I colored the methodology in blue, the conclusion in yellow and the patient types in pink. Even though I was a novice at presenting, the hiring manager admired my problem-solving skills and hired me on the spot.

Secret: Want Ads Are Used Less Than In The Past, But Still Can Spark Your Job Opportunity

Some pharmaceutical companies still place ads in major newspapers from time to time, but with the advent of company websites and online job sites, they are not used as much as they were in the past. But, a local newspaper ad was the avenue along with networking that got one of the authors her first representative job.

Lynn's Story

Life is interesting. I had not had any thoughts or knowledge of pharmaceutical sales. One day, I ran into a longtime family friend in the supermarket, who I had not seen in years. Tom told me he had been thinking of me. He ran into a former colleague who now sells pharmaceuticals and she reminded him of me. Then Tom blurted out, 'Do you know anything about pharmaceutical sales? I think you'd be good at it.' Tom and I chatted a little more and that was that.

A week or two later I was reading a magazine while getting a haircut and there was a story in it about a nurse who had become a pharmaceutical rep and more than doubled her income. A day or two later I was visiting my mother who had just returned from a doctor's appointment. She described a female rep she saw there, and said there was something about her that made her think of me.

With all these coincidences, I began thinking about pharmaceutical sales and wondered what this was all about. Meanwhile, at this time, my husband was in and out of the hospital, and I was acting as the diagnostician for his recovery from surgery and the effects of medications he was taking.

Whether it was the alignment of the stars or just coincidence, I'll never know. But I called Tom and asked for the contact information on his friend who had become a sales representative. Megan and I had coffee and she gave me a lot of the inside secrets about the business.

Shortly afterwards, I saw an ad in the Washington Post classified section for a flextime position and applied in January 1989. I followed up by calling the company. I was told my message was passed on to the area district manager. But, months passed and I heard nothing. Then, I wrote a letter to express my interest again.

Still nothing.

One evening, about six months later, around 9 p.m., I got a call from the local district manager. She wanted to know if I was still interested. I must have hesitated because she said, "Well you don't seem interested." I said, "No wait a minute. I applied in January. It's now June and it's 9 pm. I'd like to speak to you about this tomorrow."

The next day when I was fresh and alert, I was able to express my interest better. Long story, short, I got the position and continuous promotions through my fourteen-year career as a sales representative. I loved it!

Secret: Job Fairs Can Be A Good Avenue To Explore

The pharmaceutical industry does participate in job fairs at some universities for undergraduates and graduate programs. Nick's story is an example of a success story through a university job fair.

Nick's Story

I was a psychology and mental health major in college. I had always planned to be a counselor, but I soon learned that the money in this field was not what I had in mind.

I had always heard about pharmaceutical sales and that it was very hard to get into, so I never pursued it. Also, I did not have any sales experience, so I didn't think I would have a chance. I decided to go to business school and earned my MBA at University of Maryland.

Around graduation, notices for a job fair were posted and I decided to check it out. The job fair had lots of companies from technology, consulting, sales, and pharmaceuticals.

Almost without realizing it, I made a beeline for the pharmaceutical tables. Although I had no sales experience, one pharmaceutical company liked the fact that I had an MBA, interviewed me and offered me a job. The company had a great training program on the product I'd be selling but also on selling techniques. That was eight years ago, and now I am a specialty sales representative. I love the business.

Secret: Do Better "Intel" To Do Well In The Networking And Interview Process

---

Knowledge is power in any business, but none more so than the pharmaceutical business. That's why we gave you a heads up on all the code words and buzzwords that you'll be hearing. That way you'll be able to nod knowingly, and even toss in a few yourself.

But as you move forward in your job search, you'll need to do research every step of the way on the company you're meeting with and the drug and therapy area that a job opening is in. If you want to work for a specific company, you can call recruiting offices and ask to speak to the person working for Pfizer, J&J, Merck, or whatever company you're interested in.

Online Research Tools

❖ **Pharmaceutical Company Websites**
Another obvious place to go is directly to the company website. You can click through and find the area you'd like to work in and see if there are any vacancies. If there is a vacancy then you can submit your resume directly. We're not convinced this is particularly successful, but we do believe in the numbers game and think you should submit a resume here.

❖ **Google**
Google is a great resource. Go to Google and type in the company name and you'll find a wealth of information, from the company's own website to recent articles and news stories.

Researching the company you are going to interview with is a must. If you do not do the research, chances are you're not really serious about landing the job. The best place to look, of course, is the internet. Just go to the company website and learn some basic information.

The Key Information You'll Want To Gather:

- ❖ Home Office Location
  - ■ This is where you will likely go for training.

- ❖ President and Key People
  - ■ Know the name of the president of the company.
  - ■ Know who the heads of the therapy class (such as respiratory or cardiovascular) you are interviewing for. (Check to see if this information is available online.)

- ❖ Main Products
  - ■ Know something about the company's main products and the product you will be selling.
  - ■ If you are working with a recruiter or have a contact in the company, they can help you with the company's key products.

- ❖ Competitive Products
  - ■ Know who your competitors are, both the drug and the company name.
  - ■ Research competitive products online as well.

- ❖ Pipeline Products
  - ■ Know what products are currently in approval stages.
  - ■ Is there any product that the company is eagerly awaiting FDA approval on?
  - ■ The pipeline products give you some insight into the future of the company and your job.

As you go forward, the more research you do, the more impressive you will be as you meet more people in the pharmaceutical industry.

—In A Nutshell—

Have a strategy and a game plan.
Develop a network of contacts.
Focus on your best prospects and get to know them well.

4.

Define Your Experience
So *You*
Stand Out From The Crowd

"All the world's a stage,
And all the men and women merely players."
—*William Shakespeare*

Why is being different important?

Having a different pitch for yourself is powerful. It will *position* you apart from the crowd. There are many people competing for your job or your opportunity. That's why your positioning must be different from your competitors in the minds of hiring managers in the pharmaceutical industry.

Differentiation is a cardinal rule for any job search in a sought-after, well-paid arena like pharmaceutical sales. You have to stand out from the crowd. There are hundreds of other people out there vying for the same sales job you want. Hiring managers are inundated with resumes and emails for every job opening. So, when you look like everyone else, you're lost in the crowd.

When you don't have a different pitch or approach, you are a generic version of the name brand. You are colorless. You are not memorable. You are not persuasive.

When you're perceived as a generic, the only way you can compete is in terms of price—a low price. (And we doubt that selling yourself cheap is why you are attracted to this field.)

Secret: Develop Your Own USP (Unique Selling Proposition)

Getting a job in a sought-after arena is a battle of sorts. You're in battle with all the other people competing for the same thing you are. So you need to present your strengths and assets in the best possible way.

You need to come up with a compelling reason why they should hire you. What you're searching for is *your* different idea, a different idea that resonates with your target market—the hiring managers—that no one can fulfill quite the way *you* can. And, if you're savvy, you'll take your difference and market it differently than other people as well.

Hiring managers spend a lot of time on delineating differences: different benefits, different look, different message, different experience, different skill set. What they are looking for is who has the best promise—what one person has to offer that the competing people don't.

One hiring manager told us that he wanted each individual to bring some different strength to support team efforts. This philosophy was particularly helpful when Terry was selecting a new representative for his team. If he had three candidates he liked, Terry asked himself, "With all things being equal, which person brings a skill or strength to the team that we don't currently have?"

Many people shortchange themselves when it comes to targeting their USP. They don't develop their different promise and the benefit to the company they are targeting. They are busy working hard looking for a job, but it is not working smart. Don't be one of them. This exercise will get you started thinking about how you might distinguish yourself from the herd.

Exercise: Be Different Or Be Gone

Directions: This exercise is designed to get you thinking of yourself in a competitive field and to develop initial ideas about what's different about you and the benefit that brings to your job or business.

What is different about you? (Your capabilities, approach, style, credentials, passions, ideas)

_____

_____

_____

What is the benefit—your promise—that you bring to a job or project that distinguishes you from others?

_____

_____

_____

What would your friends say is your key differentiating characteristic or ability? Ask them.

_____

_____

_____

Write it down in cursive. (Remember when you write down your thoughts in cursive it engages the mind so you think of more ideas).

Look at yourself. What are your strong attributes? How do they compare with the attributes the industry prizes? How does your boss define your strengths and weaknesses? If you were a competitor, how would you critique yourself?

Secret: Do The SWOT Analysis

The SWOT (Strengths, Weaknesses, Opportunities, Threats) is a handy way marketers analyze a product or company to develop the best marketing strategy. And, it's just plain common sense. What you want to do is to challenge old assumptions about what may or may not be right about yourself and your experience. What worked in the past probably will still work this year, but you won't know for sure unless you challenge it. Today, we need to be *employable* not just employed.

Brand managers do a SWOT analysis so they can keep their brands relevant and find new opportunities. As a job seeker, you have to be relevant and find new opportunities, too. Too much of the time we have so many rules and limits that we don't see the opportunity. We don't look at our strengths and the changes going on in the world through different prisms. You can get started with your own SWOT analysis in this exercise.

Exercise: The SWOT Analysis: Strengths, Weaknesses, Opportunities, Threats

Directions: The key to getting a good result from this exercise is to not censor yourself. Right down any and all things that come to mind in each area.

SWOT Analysis

Strengths: *Write down anything that you are good at and love to do or what your boss (colleagues, clients, friends) gives you high marks on (may or may not be true) but it's how you're perceived (currently).*

Weaknesses: *Write down what you're terrible at and hate to do, or what your boss and friends criticize you for or suggest you improve.*

Opportunities: *This is wide open. Look at all the dynamics taking place in the pharmaceutical industry and at individual companies. Write down anything that could be an opportunity for you. A key is to look for unmet or unsatisfied needs that you could capitalize on in the industry.*

Threats: *Write down what keeps you awake at night, whether real or imagined, about yourself, your career or the future.*

Write it down in cursive.

"Strengths" and "Weaknesses," the first two areas, deal with you. Think of strengths as assets that could be links to your success. Assets are areas to build on. Weaknesses are areas to avoid since you are not on solid ground there. Some weaknesses may be areas to target for development if they are integral to your life strategy such as communication skills and networking.

Remember, practically anything can be a strength. Start with skills, experience and accomplishments and develop your Top Ten List of strengths. Then, expand the list to include personality traits. Expand it further to include anyone you have known or even met, and anything that you have explored and been interested in. What you are looking for is all areas that can be an asset in your quest to break into pharmaceutical sales.

The second two areas deal with "Opportunities" and "Threats" in the pharmaceutical industry you are exploring. What is going on that could dramatically change things? What is not working well? What are the issues in the pharmaceutical companies that you are exploring? (If you check individual websites and read the Sunday *New York Times*, you should be up-to-date).

Business is dynamic, and none more so than the pharmaceutical industry. It is high profile because of all the issues on healthcare, medical insurance, the cost of prescription drugs that affect each and every one of us. So there is always movement and change. There will always be things that people are frustrated with. There will always be room for new ideas. Change itself always creates new unmet or unsatisfied needs that you can take advantage of in your job quest.

What you want to do is position yourself as the right kind of sales representative that's needed in the brave new world the pharmaceutical industry is facing. You want to be the solution that solves the new needs in the pharmaceutical market.

Secret: Position Yourself As The New Breed Of Sales Person That Is Needed In Pharmaceutical Sales Today

---

The trend is clear. New approaches are needed in pharmaceutical sales. (The more you read about the industry, the more this will be apparent.)

As a pharmaceutical sales person today, you need to take an approach that is similar to the business development or marketing mindset.

We think it is important to be a person who understands business and sales, and a person who is comfortable with the world of science and healthcare.

The reason why is simple. You have two masters. You have your district manager who will be interested in the numbers you generate. And you have the physicians and healthcare providers who are interested not in numbers but science and medicine and the value you bring to them.

The key thing to remember is that you can't generate the numbers without focus on your future clients—the physicians and other healthcare providers you'll be calling on who can prescribe your drug to their patients. To succeed with them, you need to think of what they need and want, not what you want to sell them.

Today, selling is about *intellectual value.* Sales representatives need to develop programs and sales approaches that focus on the science behind a drug and how it will help an MD deliver optimal care. Selling is also about *relationships*—relationships with highly intelligent people who are attracted to science, medicine and patient health. You need to feel comfortable in that world and be interested in it, too.

The pharmaceutical industry is highly regulated and there is zero tolerance for not adhering to these guidelines, regulations, and rules. You must be very comfortable in an environment like this and convey that to the hiring manager.

In a nutshell, selling is about being the right type of representative, an effective representative who continually brings relevant clinical information to health care providers. During your job quest, establish links from your past experience that demonstrate delivering intellectual value in previous jobs.

Secret: Smart Reps Focus On Building Relationships, Not Just Closing The Sale With The MD

Traditionally, representatives had a laser focus on one person: the MD. But that's yesterday's sales model. (Luckily for you, most representatives are still doing business the old-fashioned way. Let them. You will be more successful.)

We believe representatives need to build working relationships not only with the MD, but with all the stakeholders in the medical office. After all, all of them can influence your sales success.

That means nurse practitioners (NPs) and physician's assistants (PAs). Most are licensed to prescribe drugs to patients, yet many sales representatives ignore them. Don't. They can prescribe your drug and they can influence the doctors in the office as well. Most nurse practitioners and physician's assistants are more accessible than the doctors in the office as well. Don't fall into the trap of treating NPs and PAs like second-class citizens. They can be powerful allies. (Particularly if the rep selling the competition's drug is snubbing them.)

But we also mean nurses and receptionists. Of course they can't write prescriptions, but in most offices, they are the MD's gatekeepers and they do refill prescriptions and this is valuable information for you. And we've always felt that if Dr. So and So has chosen his receptionist to be the face of his practice, you should want to work with them, too. Remember, a gatekeeper controls access, so if they want, they can shut you out. You want to be the kind of representative who builds an army of helpers in your job quest and later in the job.

You want to build relationships with everyone in the office so they are "selling" for you when you're not there. Your goal is to be top of mind for your drug, your patient education material, your professionalism, your likeability quotient, and the value you bring to all stakeholders.

Secret: Position Yourself Right So You Are What The Industry Is Looking For

---

Take a minute to think about what you will be selling. You will be selling "gold standard" and new treatment therapies for a variety of diseases. "Gold standard" refers to drugs that have been on the market for a long time and have proven themselves to be very effective and safe. Gold standard drugs are the drugs to which all others in their class are compared.

As a sales rep, your job will be to educate physicians, physician assistants, nurse practitioners, nurses, and pharmacists about your drug. All the stakeholders are highly educated and have a responsibility to deliver the best care to patients. As a rep, you will be providing relevant clinical data to help prescribers stay current with all the new information they need for this very important endeavor.

Here are some of the key traits that pharmaceutical hiring managers look for in job candidates:

❖ **Education**—A 4-year college degree is required at most companies. A science degree is good, but generally only a plus if your background includes successful sales experience. Many candidates supplement their education with accreditation or certification in the pharmaceutical industry. While education and accreditation can help you stand out from other candidates, you must convince them you can sell.

❖ **Sales Experience**—Documented sales success is a must. You must impress upon hiring managers that you can sell. This is the bottom line for getting hired.

❖ **High Energy**—You must convey an energetic spirit and a positive attitude.

❖ **Well Read**—You have to stay current on all the latest breaking news regarding your drug and disease state. This includes following the news, reading medical journals and, most importantly, reading everything your company sends you. You should emphasize your appetite for keeping up on industry news and products in your past jobs.

❖ **Articulate**—You need to be able to deliver complicated information in a clear, concise manner in a very short time. This is something you can learn to do. (We'll take you through some exercises in the chapters on interviewing to help you bone up on breaking down complicated information into a simpler sales proposition.) But you have a very tangible way to demonstrate that you are articulate in the job hunt process by writing good letters, handling yourself well on the telephone, writing concise email messages. (Take a pause, and reread your message before you hit the send button.)

❖ **Follow the Rules**—As a representative you must have a thorough understanding of all the regulations and guidelines that you need to work within. The pharmaceutical industry is a highly regulated industry and there is *zero tolerance* in all companies for not adhering to the rules.

❖ **Results**—Every sales manager is under a lot of pressure to produce sales results, and as a sales representative, you will have to deliver them for your territory. Establish links with your background that demonstrate how you are the type of person that produces results in various types of situations.

❖ **Value Added**—You always want to create the perception that you bring something extra to the party. No manager wants to hire someone whose idea of a sales representative is to just go out, drop samples and come home. One manager always asks his representatives, "What is the one gold nugget you came away with? Tell me where you are going to grow your business. What is your wish list? What's on your customer's wish list?"

❖ **Listening Skills**—Hiring managers will be observing candidates to determine how well they listen, and whether or not they can be coached to be a knowledgeable sales representative. On-going training is crucial in the pharmaceutical industry.

❖ **Follow-through**—Often you will be asked in an interview about paperwork and meeting deadlines. You will need to give examples of your ability to stay on track and on time in your work.

Secret: Think Outside—In, Not Inside—Out

The bottom line is to think Outside—In: First, think in terms of what *they* are looking for (the Outside). Then, work backwards to yourself (the Inside) and position yourself so your skills and experience are what they want.

First, who is "they"?

"They" are the resume screeners, recruiters, hiring managers and senior management of pharmaceutical companies you hope to work for.

Start with what they are looking for in job candidates (Look at the previous secrets). Analyze what you have been learning on your informational interviews and website and media "research." Then draw links with your own experiences to position yourself to have those traits and experiences.

Most people think Inside—Out: "Here's who I am and what I want" (Inside). It's just not effective. Hiring managers, recruiters and the like are in the driver's seat in the job hiring process. You have to position yourself as something they want to buy. (Think like a brand.)

Realize that there are a lot of ways you can define your experience and skills. Successful job seekers think in terms of what pharmaceutical companies and recruiters want, and how they fulfill that. They think Outside—In. Here's an exercise to get you started.

Exercise: You Define Your Career

Directions: What's important to find as you do this exercise is what others want and how they perceive you, not what you know to be true about yourself.

Write down what "They" are looking for in a pharmaceutical sales representative:

_____

_____

_____

Write down aspects of your own experience or skills that fulfill what "they" are looking for:

_____

_____

_____

Write it down in cursive.

Secret: Brand Yourself Or Be Branded

If you don't *brand* yourself, other people will brand you. People are always categorizing other people: good candidate or weak candidate, interesting background or irrelevant experience, Hire or Circular File. It's Either—Or. If not this, then the person must be that.

So you want to play an active role in defining yourself and your experience so that you are branded in a positive way. Often you can change perceptions by changing the wording in how you talk about yourself in a meeting or describe your background in your resume. (We'll talk more about resumes and the interview in the next chapters.) But you need to start paying attention to how you are perceived by others, and respond accordingly. Here is an exercise to begin.

Exercise: Brand You

Here are the five things other people would say about me:

_____

_____

_____

By next year, I will also be known for the following 2–3 things:

_____

_____

_____

Here are the things I am doing right now to brand myself better:

_____

_____

_____

Write it down in cursive.

Secret: Brand Yourself As A Super Salesperson That Can Make An Impact With Doctors

---

Many people think you need a science degree to impress a hiring manager and get a job as a sales rep. This is simply not true. While historically the industry hired pharmacists as reps, managers learned that even though they understood the drugs, most pharmacists couldn't sell. And teaching someone to sell is more difficult than teaching someone product information. Having credentials in pharmaceutical marketing can be impressive and help you stand out from the crowd, but you need to do more.

That's why you want to brand yourself as a salesperson. The key question in a hiring manager's mind is going to be: Can you sell? That is the main thing your hiring manager will care about. Everything else can be taught. So you need to demonstrate a track record in sales (more on that in the next chapter).

5 Things You Must Prove To The Hiring Manager

1. You can sell.

2. You are trainable.

3. You can be effective with doctors.

4. You are a relentless worker.

5. You've got the right personality.

The key things managers will be looking for are outlined above. They also want to make sure you have the right personality and interpersonal skills. Hiring managers must be convinced that you can make an impact with doctors and healthcare providers.

You have to be a bit of a risk taker because you're always going to have to deal with rejection and keep coming back. One way to do that is to be persistent with them! And you have to convince hiring managers that you have the confidence and intelligence to be effective in selling to doctors. That's why we think it's smart to bone up on the industry, the company and the therapy class to make a strong, positive impression.

—In A Nutshell—

You define your career.
Look for ways to be different from the herd
And to tangibly demonstrate that you can sell,
So your experience will be different from the herd.

5.

Dazzle Them With A Killer Resume And Cover Letter

"It ain't bragging if you done it."

—*Dizzy Dean*

Your resume is the first impression you make on a hiring manager or other executive at a pharmaceutical company. And we all know how lasting first impressions are. A resume is more important even than the cover letter that accompanies it. Most human resource people and hiring managers look at the resume first. Then, if the resume piques their interest, they read the cover letter (if it is still attached). Research bears this out. So pay utmost attention to crafting your resume.

Most of the resumes we come across do not present the person as well as they could. They don't make an unforgettable first impression. They are not marketing pieces. They don't sell the candidate well. They don't persuade the reader to want to meet the candidate to learn more.

Most resumes are a laundry list of skills and jobs with no focus or message. Most are boring, a high percentage are downright terrible. They are full of jargon and clichés, and look downright ugly or forbidding in terms of layout and display of the content. It is no surprise that many are deposited into the discard bin with just a quick glance. Your goal is to get your resume into the "Review further" category.

The good news is a resume can be a powerful way to position and sell yourself and create a powerful personal identity. So how do you do it? You begin by adopting the mindset we've been talking about in this book, a personal branding mindset.

❖ The first shift is from resume as job history to resume as an advertisement for the brand, *You*.

❖ The second shift you need to make is to a market orientation. Don't think of what you want to tell the pharmaceutical company, but, think of what reaction you want from them, and how best to present your resume to accomplish that response.

❖ The third shift is to focus your message. Rather than a resume as laundry list, develop a single minded positioning for yourself that differentiates you from others and is relevant to your target market. The resume should tell the story of that positioning and link the various aspects of your career in a coherent whole.

❖ The final shift is to be memorable visually and verbally. The layout should look inviting and the copy should capture the reader's attention and compel them to read more.

Secret: Develop A Compelling Personal Brand Profile At The Top Of Your Resume

---

Your profile at the top of your resume is like the headline in an ad. The profile should identify who you are, what sets you apart from others, and the value added you would bring as a pharmaceutical sales rep. A profile should not only differentiate you, it should sell with a compelling reason to choose you and not the other people you are competing against.

Resume Profile Areas:

❖ Key leadership and business accomplishments (tangible and intangible)

❖ Industry or functional experience

❖ Current title or level

❖ Quantifiable achievements: revenue generated, budgets, new business

❖ Sense of personality and leadership philosophy

❖ Years of experience (never list over 20)

❖ Companies or clients

Most importantly, stay away from the boring "Objective: seeking to obtain a challenging pharmaceutical sales position" that many people use at the top of their resumes. It's too boring and expected, and won't help persuade people to hire you. Here's how to make an impressive beginning to your resume.

"Before" Profile For A Sales Executive

John Doe

Summary
Proven sales professional with over 10 years experience
Team player with good interpersonal skills
Extensive sales experience
Excellent presentation and sales skills

There are two key problems with this profile: One, it is too generic and uses generalities and clichés we've seen before in hundreds of resumes. Secondly, it does not differentiate this sales executive from other people with similar experience.

"After" Profile

JOHN DOE
SALES LEADER * NEW BUSINESS LEADER * MOTIVATOR

EXECUTIVE PROFILE

I am a sales leader who brings innovative thinking, a results focus and a marketing orientation to building client sales. I have a strong history of leadership and innovation in sales: I have been in the top 10 percent in sales production at XYZ Company over the past five years, and the new business leader this last year. My new business focus capitalized on the changing dynamics facing the ABC industry, resulting in a 20 percent increase in sales production. *In short, I am a sales leader and innovator in new business development who is driven by challenge and the desire to add value.*

Key Changes To Profile:

Headline of personal branding statement immediately grabs attention and points out candidate's expertise and positioning:

*Sales Producer * New Business Leader* Motivator*

The positioning statement makes three key points:

Not a traditional sales person, is innovative with a marketing orientation
Points out tangible leadership accomplishments: top 10% of sales producers and last year's top sales person in new accounts
Is motivated and a motivator

Exercise: Put Together Your Resume Profile

Directions: Use this exercise to explore different words and ways of positioning yourself and your experience.

What positioning words would work best in selling you for a pharmaceutical sales rep position that relate to who you are and your experience?

Now, explore developing your positioning paragraph, an interesting way of describing yourself and your experience that will set you apart from other candidates. Look at the profile above for ideas. It is always good to end with a "sound bite" in italics at the end for the key idea you want to embed in the minds of people reading your resume.

Secret: Emphasize "Results" In Your Resume: Sales Is About Results

---

On its most basic level, selling is about results.

In looking at your resume as an "advertisement," we began with a profile that positioned you to stand out from the crowd and emphasized tangible results and achievements.

After your executive summary, you need to demonstrate your accomplishments. Accomplishments should always include results. Results are the ROI—return on investment.

Ways To Demonstrate Results:

❖ Increased sales volume of low performing territory by making one more additional cold call per day.
   Results: Sales increased from $ xxx to $xx,xxx.

❖ Signed XYZ Company to exclusive contract for five years.
   Results: XYZ Company will order all "widgets" for the next five years through us increasing territory sales 15%.

❖ Developed cold call script for my team that was successful 5 out of 10 times.
   Results: 30% increase in appointments for all sales representatives in my district resulting in increased sales of 12% in the first quarter.

You get the idea. Link your activity to outcomes in writing your resume as well as in your conversation during interviews.

Sales professionals have to have a keen understanding of what activities drive their business. Those are the only activities that really matter to hiring managers. However, sales professionals also know that there are activities, such as paper work, that need to be done because it is part of the job. In this instance, concentrate on outcomes in your resume, but certainly be able to talk about your ability to handle the softer skills such as administrative paperwork and reporting.

Exercise: Quantifying Results

Directions: When you begin writing your resume, for every job, for every project, think:

Accomplishment:

_____

_____

_____

Results:

_____

_____

_____

Write it down in cursive.

Secret: Use Action Words And Specifics To Tell A "Story"

You want your resume to paint a picture of who you are to tell a story that is memorable and persuasive to a hiring manager or recruiter. The best way to do that is to use action words and tell a story about what you did.

Of course, as we've mentioned, emphasize the tasks and skills the pharmaceutical sales job entails, such as program planning, analyzing data, setting up a territory and sample accountability. What do you do in your current job that demonstrates your skills and expertise in these areas?

Examples That Tell A Story:

❖ Challenged to fuel growth for failing financial services product in a climate beset by poor internal morale and declining revenue. Based on my team's analysis of the research data, refocused business around new application for the product that led to exceeding $50 million budget goal.

❖ An outside-the-box thinker who has personally conceived and developed innovative new business pitches that have generated more then $5 million in new accounts.

❖ Sales person who is more customer-focused than the customer. Leave no stone unturned, front end and back end, to maximize customer lifetime value. Strategies have increased lifetime value 100%+.

❖ A people motivator who encourages colleagues and staff to grow in new directions and try new solutions. Last year, my team was responsible for increasing business revenue 50% over the previous year by leveraging client contacts to gain access to new decision-making areas.

❖ Established new sales territory for company products in Silicon Valley, developing new accounts in technology companies from small start-ups just one step up from the garage to well-known tech brand names.

Secret: Take A Page From Advertising And Use A Celebrity Endorsement

---

We're not talking about real celebrities here. We don't know any, and you probably don't either. "Celebrity" in this case is a manager, senior executive or client that you worked with who has agreed to provide a third part endorsement. Having a short quote from a boss or satisfied client is a remarkable way to get your resume to stand out, and you'll be surprised how many people will agree to be quoted if you ask them. You can place the senior executive endorsement in a Leadership or Achievement Addendum at the end of the resume, or place it right after your profile statement at the beginning of your resume.

Endorsement From Previous Boss:

VP Sales Comments:
John is exceptional at team building and sales leadership, guiding team members and executives in reaching or exceeding goals. His charisma and ability to motivate a wide range of sales professionals helped the company achieve and often exceed budget goals.

> ## Secret: Bowl Them Over With A Compelling Achievement Addendum

A page with achievements or leadership initiatives as an addendum is a relatively new device used by senior executives to set their accomplishments apart and serve as the "clincher" in the sale. A resume can do a lot in selling you, but an Achievement Addendum is the something more than often makes the critical difference is choosing you, and not the other guy.

Putting together an Achievement Addendum demands some intense work on your part, in identifying career defining achievements, things you have done that meant a lot to you, help define you, and are compelling to the people you are trying to impress at pharmaceutical companies. The Achievement Addendum should be an interesting read and tell the story of your career accomplishments. Because it doesn't have all the usual resume trappings, it can be highly effective in putting your resume to the top of the pile. Chances are most of your competitors won't have one, which is good for you. You want to stand apart from the herd.

Format For Achievement Addendum:

❖ Headline the top of the page with something like: "Critical Leadership Initiatives" or "Key Sales Achievements" or another title that works for your background.

❖ The key goal is using this section to tell a story of how you as an executive or a professional solved problems and saved the day (made money or saved money, etc.).

❖ Formats that work well are a small story setup, followed by a "Results" paragraph and a "Strengths" paragraph, or a "Challenge", followed by "Action" and "Results."

Sample Leadership Addendum:

Increased revenue 25% through opening up new business segment.

Challenge: As Director of Sales for ABC, needed to dramatically increase revenue in the X marketplace. Pursued a new contract with XYZ Company to make ABC's new software part of their product offering. Worked closely with engineering and technology departments to design and cost out product.

Results: $5 million contract was the second largest in the company's history, and led to a profitable on-going relationship. Contract generated publicity in the trade press.

Strengths: "I am the salesperson's salesperson. I love the challenge of breaking new ground in sales and negotiating the impossible contract."

You should prepare a resume template that is your working document. You can customize it based on the company you are meeting with, and update it as your career expands. Notice what people respond to in your resume when you meet with pharmaceutical executives. These are the areas to emphasize in your template as you go forward. Remember, a resume is your first impression, and for most people, it is the lasting impression. Make your resume a memorable one.

Secret: Write A Compelling Cover Letter To Accompany Your Resume

---

Remember when you write your cover letter during the job search process, that you are writing to another human being.

Obvious? Well, maybe not.

Many of the cover letters that we have seen are so stilted and institutional, that they are not effective. Don't misunderstand. It is important to be professional and polite. But, you don't want to sound like a machine, either. You are a live person who is writing a letter to begin a relationship, hopefully a profitable, long-term career relationship. You want to be clear and use a conversational tone. A good rule of thumb is to write like you are talking to a business colleague.

Do's And Don'ts Of Writing Good Cover Letters:

❖ **Don't Send Every Pharma Company The Same Letter.** Generic letters read like generic letters. Work from your Focus List, the group of companies you are targeting and know something about. Tell them why you are interested in that company.

❖ **Do Write To A Specific Person.** Never write to "The Hiring Manager." Locate a name.

❖ **Don't Misspell Names.** It is worth a phone call if you can't get it any other way. A misspelled name can be the kiss of death with some managers, and it happens all the time.

❖ **Do Give A Compelling Sales Pitch.** The pitch should be a short description of your defining qualities and experiences. Say why you are interested in pharmaceutical sales and what you can bring to the job. In short, why they should hire you and not the next resume in the pile. (Look at the theme you developed in your resume profile statement.)

❖ **Be Natural And Engaging.** Don't write to an institution. Write like you are talking to a friend or colleague.

❖ **Personalize The Letter.** If it is through a colleague or doctor, say, "So and So suggested that I contact you." If you can't personalize the letter in that way, write the letter in a personal, yet professional style.

❖ **Limit It To One Page.** People in pharma are busy, so you need to be able to write an articulate one-page letter that does the job.

Secret: No Matter What Happened At The Meeting, Always Write A Follow-up Letter Or Email

---

Since you want to build a broad network of contacts in the pharmaceutical business, never pass up the opportunity to nurture relationships through contact of some sort. The more you touch base with new people you meet, the more memorable you will be. As long as you don't hound people, you will be viewed as having good pharma sales potential.

No matter what happened in the meeting, you need to follow up with an interesting letter or email within two or three days of the meeting. Use this opportunity to talk specifically about the meeting and the business issues that were discussed. You may want to put in some possible solutions. Talk about your skills and qualifications in a sentence or two. As in the cover letter and all your business correspondence for that matter, write in a conversational style as you would to a business colleague you like.

The trick is to write a winning letter that has a sense of excitement to it—to be engaging so that the pharma manager wants to know more. We know it's not easy, but try to have this goal in mind.

To do this, you might bring up some experience you have that relates to your in-person meeting that you didn't bring up at the time. (Most of us have lots of ideas on how we could have handled a question after the fact). The reaction you want is for them to want to know more about you, to pass you along to the next person in the interview process. You letters and emails will help paint a picture of you as the type of rep that is right for the hiring manager's team.

—In A Nutshell—

Your resume and letter are the first impression you make. Make it a lasting impression that sells you.

6.

Make A Great First Impression In The Interview

*"Who you are speaks so loudly
I can't hear what you're saying"*

—*Ralph Waldo Emerson*

We are pegged in the first few minutes of an interview, sometimes in a matter of seconds. Good Fit—Poor fit. Hire—Not hire. Professional—Disorganized. Successful—Unsuccessful. Like—Dislike.

It all happens quickly. Many recruiters and hiring managers have secretly described it to us. The job candidate is barely in the door, and already has been sized up, maybe even eliminated as a contender for the job. A hiring manager has made up his or her mind about the job prospect, what they are like (even what they are worth) and the candidate has barely said a word.

It's all based on our snap impression: how a new job candidate enters the room, how they look, their clothes, how they carry themselves, their body language or their actual language—the way they speak.

It happens all the time. One pharmaceutical hiring manager told us, "Interviewing people is quite an eye opener. The impression made within the first one to two minutes is unmistakable. Rarely does it change as the interview moves forward. I am always amazed at the number of candidates who come unprepared, don't bring anything to take notes, and then ask me at the end of the interview what they should send back."

The power of a first impression isn't anything particular about the pharmaceutical industry. In fact, if we're honest, we're all guilty of making snap judgments about new people we meet.

Self-presentation—the way you look and present yourself—is important because of the link that people make between what something looks like on the outside and what is on the inside. Despite familiar admonitions like "Don't judge a book by its cover," the fact is that most of us do just that.

How do you look and carry yourself? What are the messages there? Are you packaging yourself as well as you might? What do you *want* your entire "package" to say about you? Are you prepared with "extras" that can help you make a great first impression in an interview?

The secrets in this chapter will show you how to make a great impression in the pharmaceutical industry. You want to create a strong visual and verbal identity for yourself. To do that, you must think about the way you dress, have a focused message that's different and relevant, and bring a Brag Book to the interview.

Secret: Dress For Success In The Pharmaceutical Industry

The pharmaceutical industry is conservative compared to other industries. Men should wear a conservative suit or sports jacket, slacks and a tie. Women should wear a conservative suit with slacks or skirt. Either is appropriate.

Whether you are a woman or a man, you can never go wrong with a quality navy suit. We know a district manager who once said she would never hire a woman who wore a red suit to an interview. "Why?" we asked. The DM replied, "Because red is the color of power and I will assume her real goal is getting my job." Now this is only one manager out of hundreds if not thousands who might feel this way, but the story underscores our point that the pharmaceutical industry is more traditional and conservative than other fields. You should really think about what you wear to the interview and what message you want to convey.

You not only want to look like a professional, you should bring your professional tools, such as your appointment book or PDA. It could help you stand out. Organization is a key component of any sales job. The more organized you are, the more efficient you are likely to be. This also points to efficient and timely follow-up with customers, a critical component of successful selling. You want to be prepared to schedule the next meeting. You'll come across as a sales amateur if you aren't prepared to schedule a follow-up meeting.

Remember, your interview is a sales call. Treat it as such. You are selling yourself and how your USP will be a good fit for this manager and the team you will be joining. Be prepared and polished.

> ## Secret: Have A 30-Second Elevator Speech That Sells You As A Hot Pharmaceutical Sales Prospect

Your "elevator speech" is a short pithy description of who you are, what's different about you, and the extra value you would bring to the job as a sales rep in the pharmaceutical industry.

Why do you need an elevator speech?

In a nutshell, an elevator speech will help you to be remembered and stand out from the competition. The people you will be interviewing with are meeting lots of job candidates. You need to give them a "sound bite" that positions you better for the job than other contenders.

Rules Of A Good Elevator Speech:

❖ **Be Short.** About the time it takes to go up 4 or 5 flights in an elevator— that's why it's called an elevator speech.

❖ **Be Memorable.** You might try to prepare a sound bite or unusual expression if you're good at that sort of thing.

❖ **Give a Compelling Reason Why *You* Should be Hired.** It is a verbal version of the profile statement at the top of your resume.

❖ **Appear Natural and Spontaneous.** Of course, it isn't. You have probably been practicing it for weeks. So this is the tricky part. You need to practice it so that it is "conversational" and flows and doesn't appear rehearsed.

Sample Elevator Speech

I'm Sally Q. One way I think of myself is as a sales person who's more customer-focused than my customers. And my clients at ABC Widgets have paid me back with their loyalty. I not only have a strong retention rate with existing clients, client referrals are my biggest source of new business. That's why I have been the top sales person at ABC Widgets for two of the last five years. Now, I'm looking for a new challenge as a pharmaceutical sales representative. I have been interested in science and medicine since high school when I was involved in community service at a local hospital. So, I'd be able to combine my two loves: medicine and building strong client relationships.

The elevator speech should be a nutshell description of who you are, but it should be said in such a way that it leads to further conversation. You don't want to halt the conversational flow of the meeting as you try to remember it. Practice so that it comes out naturally, and is a statement you feel comfortable with.

Secret: Bring A Brag Book To The Interview

We are always asked about the Brag Book, "Do I really need one?"

Yes. Yes. Yes! You appear unprepared without one. Many managers have said to us, "The interview is over in my mind if a candidate doesn't bring a Brag Book. I continue the interview out of courtesy and to pass time until my next candidate arrives." So what you bring is as important as what you say. Buy a nice binder to present a compelling story of your career and to showcase your best work so that you can present it in interviews.

Key Elements In A Brag Book:

Resume
Don't just assume that since you faxed it or emailed it, you don't need to bring a resume to each interview. The manager may be working with a poorly faxed copy or a printout from an email. Some managers ask to see your resume as a test to see how prepared you are for the meeting. So don't come empty handed. Always bring a clean, clear copy of your resume printed on good quality paper.

Letters of Recognition, Performance Appraisals
This is the "meat" of the Brag Book, so get a nice binder to showcase your best work and make a good presentation. Include letters of recognition, sales results, good performance reviews and sales contests awards. You can include special projects in an Achievement Addendum as we outlined in the previous chapter, or place them on a separate page in the Brag Book.

The rule of thumb is to include anything that demonstrates your leadership qualities. Include copies of your most recent performance appraisals. You will likely be asked for these at some point, so go ahead and offer them.

Letters You Have Written In Recognition Of Others
The pharmaceutical sales representative works as a part of a team, so demonstrating that you are a team player is very important. We think it's smart to include letters you may have written to others, such as subordinates or colleagues, for a job well done. This will demonstrate your writing ability as well as how you relate to and work with others.

Map Of The Territory You'd Be Covering
Have a map of the territory. Few candidates will bring one to the interview, so you will really stand out. Most important, you will impress the hiring manager!

And be prepared to talk about the following aspects of the territory:
- ❖ Boundaries
- ❖ Furthest points
- ❖ Closest points
- ❖ Location of your home

Once you find out where the territory is, just go out and buy a regular map at a gas station. For example, it might be a Manhattan territory with some northern suburbs. You outline the boundaries with a marker, and show where you live in relation to the entire territory.

Typically, a representative lives inside the territory. That's why it is a real advantage to demonstrate this fact at the interview. The thinking is that if a representative has to drive an hour just to get into the territory, they'll cut their workday short and count the driving as work time. Basically, hiring a rep who lives too far outside the territory is unproductive. Anecdotes prove this to be true. Too much windshield time depletes energy and enthusiasm for the job.

Put all of these materials into a nice binder and be prepared to leave several copies at each interview. Sometimes a manager will bring a sales trainer with them into new candidate interviews, so bring extra copies of your Brag Book. We recommend bringing two or three copies to each interview. Always be prepared to meet another person who will contribute to the selection process.

Be prepared at some appropriate point in the interview to walk the interviewer through your Brag Book. Don't just leave it on the table at the end of the interview. Make the interview interactive and show off your selling skills by using your Brag Book to sell yourself.

Secret: Bowl Your Interviewer Over With A Sample Selling Tool

The interview is an opportunity to show that you can sell. To do that, nothing beats a demonstration. That's why we think it is smart interviewing to bring a sample selling tool to demonstrate this core skill of sales success.

As a person trying to stand out in the interview process, what better way to show initiative than taking the interviewer through a sales piece?

If you have a sales aid that is particularly good and can be used to demonstrate your selling skills and style, use it to toot your own horn. For example, you can use a sales aid from your current job if you are a sales person. If you developed the sales tool, by all means use it to demonstrate your initiative and creativity.

However, tell the interviewer that you know this industry is highly regulated. And, you know that you cannot create your own sales pieces. You are merely showing this to demonstrate initiative and creativity.

Secret: Tell Stories About Your Experiences

What is the point of communication if we don't have an impact on the listener?

Interviews are a stage in which most people communicate poorly because they are nervous and launch into a laundry list of accomplishments. The key elements you need to think about before each interview are what you want to say, how you will say it, and how can you connect with the audience.

Stories are very powerful. That's why throughout history, stories and parables have been used to communicate ideas and move audiences. You can sell your background and accomplishments much more effectively through stories than a bullet point list of accomplishments. Paint a picture of your accomplishments in their minds.

Story Ideas You Might Want To Prepare:

- ❖ The Story Of My Greatest Job Success
- ❖ How I Was A Hero To My Client
- ❖ When I Came Up With An Idea That Was A Roaring Success
- ❖ My David And Goliath Story
- ❖ My Biggest Mistake
- ❖ The Impossible Project

With stories like these you can create a memorable impression and begin to build a relationship with the audience, in this case, the people interviewing you who you want to be a future audience as well.

—In A Nutshell—

The interview is a chance to make a great first impression.
Make it a positive, lasting impression.

7.

Prepare To
Ace The Interview

"Be prepared."

—Boy Scout motto

While interviewing well may be an art, interviewing in the pharmaceutical business is a process. You'll have phone interviews. You'll have in-person interviews. You'll have team interviews. You might be directed to the company website to respond to questions online or take a personality assessment, Myers-Briggs, for example.

So, to do interviewing well in this industry, you will need preparation. Lots of preparation, maybe even over-preparation.

Why is the interview process so intense?

Well, think about it. You will be selling million and billion dollar products. You are the face of the company to the medical community. You will be the liaison between the customer and management.

You are given a company car to drive, a laptop computer, a printer, a scanner and other office items for use in your home. You will be set up with a DSL connection. You will know about the company's proprietary marketing strategies. You will be managing thousands of dollars of samples. You will be entrusted with a budget to run your territory. You will be given a company credit card for expenses. Needless to say, you will have a lot of responsibility, so pharmaceutical companies have set up an elaborate process to find qualified representatives.

If you're like most people, the thing you most want to know before an interview is, "What kinds of questions will I be asked?" Because there are so many phases before you get that job offer, one thing is certain. You will be asked a lot of questions. We're going to include many of them in this chapter.

It helps a lot if you know what interview method the pharmaceutical company is using. You can try to find out through the network of pharmaceutical representatives and recruiters you've been cultivating. If they know, they'll be glad to tell you about it.

If you don't find out about the interviewing method through networking, this chapter will prepare you for the most common method, called STAR, that many pharmaceutical companies are using. Of course, some are still using the "Tell me about yourself" approach or other questions. The secrets in this chapter will help you ace the questions and the interview process.

Secret: Prepare For The Multiple Stages Of The Pharmaceutical Interview Process

---

When you are offered a job in pharmaceutical sales, you will feel that you have really earned it. The process is intense and the questions thought-provoking. Questions are asked for a variety of reasons. Interviewers want to learn how you think and to see how you sell. They want to see how you react under pressure. And you'll face many phases of interviews. Here is a typical interview scenario you might face.

Typical Pharmaceutical Interview Process:

<u>Phase 1: Initial Screening</u>
- ❖ Telephone or Online Interview
- ❖ Recruiter or Group of District Managers

<u>Phase 2: Hiring Manager Interviews</u>
- ❖ Hiring Manager or Group of District Managers
- ❖ Hiring Manager with Trainer or Hospital Representative

<u>Phase 3: Home Office Interviews</u>
- ❖ Regional Director
- ❖ V.P. Sales

Phase 1 interviews are to screen candidates to select ones who are a potential fit. Most interviews at this stage are to determine whether you have the minimum qualifications to do the job, and are a potential fit for the company.

Usually, a candidate is first interviewed by a recruiter in person or over the phone. Some companies have set up a group of DMs who do all the first in-person interviews. The DM committee decides if you are a fit and then sends you to the hiring manager.

After the initial screening, you move on to Phase 2, the hiring manager, the person you will work for if you land the job. The hiring manager interviews you first, one-on-one, to focus on whether you can do the job and if you're a good fit for the job and the company.

If the hiring manager is interested, the hiring manager brings you back for a group interview with a trainer or hospital representative. In this meeting, you'll be asked to present using a sales piece, called detailing. You'll detail using whatever sales piece they provide. Afterwards, the people in the meeting will rate you. (We'll go into detailing in the next chapter so that you will be prepared to handle this part of the interview.)

Once the hiring manager and the DM have decided you are the one for the job, you go to Phase 3. You will go to the home office to be interviewed by the Regional Director and VP of Sales. This phase is about getting the stamp of approval. But don't be overconfident. There will be lots of serious interview questions, as you'll see. While all of this is going on, the company will be checking your driving record and credit history. Most companies also check for a criminal record.

Believe it or not, this interview process is repeated throughout your career whenever you are being considered for a promotion. You will have to prove yourself over and over again.

Secret: Have A Good Answer For Two Fundamental Questions

As you meet the hiring managers, recruiters, DMs, RMs and other pharmaceutical executives on your job search, you'll have a lot of questions hurled at you. But two will keep cropping up again and again.

The Two Most Asked Questions:

❖ Why do you want to get into pharmaceutical sales?
❖ Why do you want to work for XYZ Company?

There is no one right answer to either question. And, of course, the real question behind all interview questions is, "What can you do for us?"

But you should prepare well for both questions in advance of your interviews. Your answer to why you want to get into pharmaceutical sales should be very personal but also have a business reason. What we mean by that is, tie your story to a benefit for the company. Your answer should also tie into your resume profile and your 30-second elevator speech.

When one person we know was asked, "Why do you want to get into pharmaceutical sales?" she said the following:

"My background is selling sophisticated tech equipment to senior executives. I like selling to highly educated people. Doctors are like that, too. I like the level of professional I would be selling to."

Another said, "I work well in a very dynamic, changing environment. I am a voracious reader and am keeping up with issues and changes the industry faces. I believe I can make a solid contribution to this industry."

Here are some answers to the second question, "Why do you want to work for this company?" that worked. (They got the job.)

"I have some personal experience with ABC disease and I know that it is not treated aggressively enough. Your company sells a drug for this disease and I believe I could bring a perspective to prescribers that would encourage them to treat it more aggressively and therefore prescribe more of your drug."

Or you could say, "I've researched the company and learned that...."

Whatever you say, it will go over best if your answer has a good business reason like the examples above.

Secret: Prepare For A STAR Interview

Many pharmaceutical companies are using an interview method that is based on the STAR Process

STAR Process—Situation Or Task, Action, Result Or Outcome

STAR is a good process both for the interviewer (always the better role in this situation) and for the interviewee, because even if traditional questions are asked, you can frame your responses better. Also, we're going to take you through the STAR method so you can prepare responses prior to the interview.

The STAR process is based on behavior theory. The belief behind this method is that the most accurate predictor of future performance is past performance in similar situations. This method focuses on experiences, behaviors, knowledge, skills and abilities that are job-related. Employers determine which skill sets are necessary for the job and ask pointed questions to determine if the candidate possesses those skills

Examples Of STAR Questions:

Situation: Give an example of a situation you were involved in that resulted in a positive outcome.

or

Task: Describe the tasks involved in that situation.

Action: Talk about the various actions involved in the situation's task.

Results: What results directly followed because of your actions?

3 Steps To STAR Questions:

❖ Describe the situation or task in detail.
❖ Describe the action you took.
❖ Describe the results (tangible or intangible).

All questions are seeking to uncover something specific to the pharmaceutical sales position; before you respond, try to clarify what that is in your mind.

In behavioral interviewing, it is critical that you listen very carefully to the questions asked so that you understand what the question is trying to uncover. Clarify if you need to. When you respond, you must be detailed and specific and refer to actual experiences. Do not leave out anything in your story. Do not assume the interviewer will connect the dots. It is your responsibility to connect the dots for them.

Situation Or Task Questions Sound Like:

Describe a situation where you were confronted with a personal conflict with a colleague. How was it resolved?

This question is trying to uncover how well you work with a team—remember pharmaceutical representatives all work in teams and conflict comes up frequently.

To Answer This Question, You Would:

Recount the situation—One of our team members had been out frequently for personal reasons and communication began to break down.

Talk about the action—You organized lunch meetings to bring the team together face to face and share information

Give the result—Morale and communication improved dramatically.

Before responding to these questions, think situation or task, the action you took, and the results or outcome. You are essentially saying, "This is what happened, this is what I did, and this is the result."

Action Questions Sound Like:

What did you do to prepare for this interview?

Take the interviewer through all of the actions you took, from learning about the day-to-day life of a pharmaceutical sales representative to the skill sets needed to do the job.

Compare your background to uncover your USP and what you bring to the table.

Describe what you did, from researching the company, networking, mapping out your territory, to putting together your Brag Book.

Talk "Outside—In." Show your skill set fits with the pharmaceutical sales representative job.

Take the interviewer step-by-step through exactly what you did. (What you did first, second, etc.)

Results Or Outcomes Questions Sound Like:

What was the result?

Was your action successful?

If no, how did you handle that?

Results questions are looking for the ROI, the return on investment of your actions, both tangible and intangible. Be specific.

If the action was not successful or as successful as you had planned, talk about what you learned and how you applied your learning to a new or different action.

In Short:

Situation Or Task Questions Sound Like:
- ❖ Describe a situation when…
- ❖ Why did you…
- ❖ What were the circumstances…

Action Questions Sound Like:
- ❖ What did you do?
- ❖ Describe specifically how….
- ❖ What did you do first…second…

Results Or Outcomes Questions Sound Like:
- ❖ What was the result?
- ❖ Was your action successful?
- ❖ If not, how did you handle that?

Example Of STAR Answers:

Situation: "During my internship last winter, I was responsible for managing various events, such as large educational conferences."

Task: "Attendance at these events had dropped by 35% over the past two years and I wanted to do something to improve these numbers."

Action: "The actions I took had dramatic results. I designed a new promotional packet that was more effective in selling our conferences and distributed it to our target businesses. Since we had no feedback on our conferences, I also included an evaluation sheet to collect feedback to use for future events. I also organized internal discussions to share these issues with our employees."

Result: "We all agreed we needed to be more customer-focused and provide more of what the customer wanted at the conferences. We utilized some of the wonderful ideas we received, and made our internal systems more efficient. Best of all, we raised attendance by 17% the first year."

Secret: Prepare Answers To The Most Likely Questions

We're going to give you a lot of questions that people have come up against in job interviews. Prepare your answers prior to the interview and you'll be ready for just about anything.

But don't just write out what your response would be. Practice *saying* the answers out loud. You'll be saying the answers in the interview, so that is how you want to practice them.

Possible Interview Questions:

- ❖ Tell me a little about yourself.
- ❖ Why do you think you will be good in this job?
- ❖ What are your three key strengths?
- ❖ Do you prefer to work with people, ideas, data or things?
- ❖ How did you learn about our company?
- ❖ Why should we hire you?
- ❖ Tell me what this job is about and your definition of a good sales representative.
- ❖ Why are you interested in working for a pharmaceutical company?
- ❖ What are you looking for in this job?
- ❖ What do you like most about this job? Least?
- ❖ Why are you switching jobs?
- ❖ What would you like to be doing five years down the road?
- ❖ What are your future goals? How will you achieve them?
- ❖ Tell me the hardest job you ever had.
- ❖ What was your biggest failure? How did you handle it?
- ❖ What else do you think we should know about you?
- ❖ What is your selling style?
- ❖ If you could start your career all over again, what would you do?
- ❖ Define what doing a great job means to you.
- ❖ What job experiences were especially satisfying?
- ❖ What key trends do you see happening in the pharmaceutical industry?

❖ How do you perceive your current employer?

❖ Describe your ideal working environment.

❖ How would your current boss describe you? Your subordinates? Your clients? Your colleagues?

❖ Describe a time your work was criticized. How did you handle that?

❖ Describe your personality.

❖ What type of relationship do you have with your boss? Your colleagues?

❖ We're looking for someone who can work independently. What experiences do you have working by yourself?

❖ If you were us, why should we choose you?

❖ What problems do you see as key in this job? How would you resolve them?

❖ What responsibilities would you like to avoid in your next job?

❖ What type of environment suits you best?

❖ What would you do if someone asked you to do something unethical?

❖ What job gave you the most personal satisfaction and why?

❖ Have you worked as a member of a team in the past? How so?

❖ What have you done that was innovative in a job?

❖ If you could change anything in your career, what would you do differently the second time around?

❖ What type of approach do you take to solving problems?

❖ What do you see as the key challenges to a pharmaceutical sales representative?

❖ When you're taking on a new assignment, do you like a lot of feedback or a lot of autonomy?

❖ Have you ever worked in a very fast-paced environment? Describe times when you worked under pressure or met deadlines.

❖ If you could do anything in the world, what would it be?

❖ Tell us about your relationship with your personal doctor.

❖ How good are you at details? Paperwork?

❖ What is a great thing a prior employer did that you wish every company did?

❖ What in your career have you been the most proud of?

❖ What do you think you'll get in this job that you don't have in your current job?

❖ Describe a job experience in which you were too persistent. What was the outcome?

❖ Talk about the biggest sale you ever made.

❖ Tell us about a major conflict with a colleague. How did you solve it?

❖ Give an example of a time when you consulted with your boss before taking action.

Reminder: Write down the answers to each question in cursive. Expand on what you might say. Then practice saying each aloud, so that the answer sounds natural, not rehearsed. When you practice, pretend that you are talking to a friend so that you bring your experience to life as you answer the question.

Secret: Don't Think WIFM; Think WIFT

Many sales professionals fall into the trap of thinking WIFM (What's in it for me?). Will I be able to get my message out in the time allotted? What did I talk about in the last interview? When will they make the decision about hiring me?

Notice how the "I's" have it? As you consider *your* agenda, how much thought do you give to WIFT (What's in it for them?).

As we said, the question behind all interview questions is, "*What can you do for us at ABC pharmaceutical company?*"

This is a very important concept in selling and developing a business relationship. After all, people buy based on what's in it for them, not what's in it for you. So yes, your agenda is an important first step to preparing for the interview, but always go one step further and consider the WIFT. This is what will really make the sale and begin the process of developing a business relationship.

Secret: Learn The Do's Of Good Interviewing

Do's For Interviewing:

❖ **Research the company.** Check out the company website, Google, recruiters and your network.

❖ **Research the hiring manager and other executives if possible.** Try asking the recruiter, your network or even checking through Google.

❖ **Practice all your interview answers aloud.** Keep your answers short and crisp.

❖ **Practice STAR interview questions and answers.** Think situation or task, action I took, solution and results.

❖ **Prepare a 30-second elevator speech.** This is a short commercial on why you are right for the job.

❖ **Link your background.** Demonstrate why you'd be good in the job of a pharmaceutical sales representative based on previous things you've done.

❖ **Be enthusiastic.** Sit up straight and give positive body language.

❖ **Ask the interviewer to explain a question.** If you are not sure what she or he wants to know, ask the interviewer to explain it. It shows that you are confident.

❖ **Have questions that you plan to ask the interviewer.** Have two to three questions. These will change as you progress through the phases of the interview process.

❖ **Focus on your message.** Have a crisp answer to why you want the job and what's in it for them.

❖ **Don't be too nervous.** Remember you have a lot to offer and you have prepared well for the interview.

—In A Nutshell—

Interviewing is an art and a process.
The key is preparation.
Link your background to
what the company needs.

8.

Be Able To Present A Detail Piece, A Clinical Paper And A PI

"Tell me, I'll forget.
Show me, I may remember.
But involve me and I'll understand."

—*Chinese proverb*

At some point in your interviews you will likely be asked to present a pharmaceutical sales aid called a detail piece, a package insert called a PI and a clinical paper. Don't panic. First of all, if you've reached this point, you're really doing well in the interviewing process. You are one of the chosen. You are being seriously considered for a job offer. When you are asked to present at most companies, it's a tangible check of your sales skills before being sent to upper management for approval. It doesn't mean you have the job, though. If you bungle your sales aid presentation, you could doom your candidacy. You don't need to be perfect at it, but your interviewers need to see that you can be trained in presenting pharmaceutical products. In this chapter, we will take you through the fine points of all three items so that you can sail through this part of the interview.

If you have been in sales, you know that presenting is really a performance. Even before you launch into the key points you want to make about the product, you are selling. So, you need to demonstrate confidence from the very moment you enter the room. Everything you say and do can help you or hurt you in terms of making the sale. You need to have all your selling materials ready and organized. When you're presenting a sales piece, you will be playing the role of the rep, and the other person will be playing the role of the physician.

Get off to a good start by making eye contact and smiling. It will help you connect with the interviewer, and increase your effectiveness immensely. If you are in a group interview, you need to connect with one person at a time as you go through your presentation. Make sure you don't spend all your time focused on the most senior person in the room. In most pharmaceutical companies, all the attendees will have a vote, and if you ignore someone, it could be to your peril.

Secret: Ask If You Should "Present The Detail Piece" Or "Make A Sales Call"

You will be given a sales aid or detail piece (as they are commonly called in the industry) and asked to take some time to review it and come back and present to the hiring manager or group of interviewers.

At this point, make sure you ask:

❖ Do you want me to *present the detail piece?*

   Or

❖ Do you want me to *make a sales call?*

This is a very important question. There is a difference between how you would set up a sales call that's different from talking through the detail piece.

—In A Nutshell—

A sales call involves probing before presenting the detail piece or sales aid. **Presenting the detail piece** involves talking through the marketing message from start to finish.

How to present the detail piece can be a stumbling block in interviews. One manager handed an interviewee a detail piece and asked the person to come back and present it to him. As the candidate told us, "Clearly, the manager wanted to see how quickly I could read and understand the information, come back and talk about it in an articulate manner. So I did that."

Afterwards, the manager said "You didn't even ask me if I used your drug. You may not have needed to go through the detail piece at all." The candidate responded by telling the manger that he did not ask her to make a sales call. Rather, he asked her to present the detail piece. Luckily, this was an enlightened manager who was big enough to agree that he had not been clear in his request.

The moral of the story is pay attention to all the nuances during the interview. Ask questions. Clarify what the manager is asking. Don't be afraid to explain why you approached something the way you did. It will make you look good because you'll appear confident. (And confidence is what they are looking for in a sales rep.)

Secret: Practice Selling From A Detail Piece

The sales aid or detail piece tells the features and benefits about the product. Detail pieces are very similar. (We have a sample detail piece for our fictional *XYZ Eye Drops* in the Appendix of the book.) The important marketing points are in *bold print*. These are the *key words* you need to use when you role-play presenting the detail piece in the interview.

Here's how it usually works in an interview. You'll be given a detail piece and given some time to practice in a separate room. When you come back to the interview room, make eye contact and begin going through the points in bold type, occasionally stopping to point out some specific clinical information in a chart.

It's important to point out some clinical data. Don't worry if you don't understand what is being said. You don't need to have a thorough understanding to be able to talk about it. You'll be trained once you land the job.

The summary of the marketing message is at the bottom of a one page sales aid or at the back of a multiple page sales aid. Use the summary to guide you through as you role-play doing a sales call in the interview.

Look at the detail piece for *XYZ Eye Drops* at the back of the book. You can immediately see the key points in the marketing message: "once a day," "safe," and "effective." This message is reflected throughout the detail piece. Notice words such as "quick response" and "pediatric use" (anything for pediatric use is very safe).

It's very effective to relate all the product features to patient benefits. For example, look at the dosing for *XYZ Eye Drops* in the sample detail piece. Once a day dosing is a feature of *XYZ Eye Drops*. You just need one drop a day compared to four or five drops a day for competitive eye drops. The benefit for the patient is convenience. *XYZ Eye Drops* are also approved for pediatric use. The benefit for the patient is safety. The next exercise takes you though a role-play presenting a detail piece so that you'll be comfortable doing it in the interview.

Exercise: Role-Play For The Detail Piece

Directions: Here is a sample role-play to practice before interviews.

Rep: *Doctor, when your patients need a quick response to dry, itchy eyes, think <u>XYZ Eye Drops</u> first. <u>XYZ Eye Drops</u> are dosed once a day which means it is very convenient for all patients and it is approved for pediatric use which means it is safe enough for patients as young as 1 year old. Studies have shown <u>XYZ Eye Drops</u> provide the greatest improvement in dry eyes within the first 48 hours of treatment. Doctor, have you had the opportunity to prescribe <u>XYZ Eye Drops</u>?*

Doctor: *No, I've been using Competitor B.*

Rep: *What do you like about Competitor B?*

Doctor: *Nothing in particular, it's probably more habit than anything special about the product.*

Rep: *Habits are a challenge to break. But your patients may find <u>XYZ Eye Drops</u> are easier to use. Dosing is once a day compared to four times a day for Competitor B. Have any of your patients told you they forget to use their eye drops?*

Doctor: *Yes, patients have complained about forgetting. Compliance is an issue with eye drops.*

Rep: *<u>XYZ Eye Drops</u> offer a much more convenient dosing schedule for patients and in a three week, well-controlled trial, 98% of patients experienced relief of dry eye symptoms within 48 hours.*

Doctor: *Mmm.*

Rep: *So, Doctor, what do you think about this information?*

Doctor: *Interesting.*

Rep: *<u>XYZ Eye Drops</u> offer your patients a fast onset of action, once daily dosing, and is safe enough for pediatric use. Doctor, do you think your patients would prefer a more convenient dosing schedule with a fast onset of action for their dry, itchy eyes?*

Doctor: *Probably, but what about managed care? Is it covered?*

Rep: *I'm glad you asked that.* <u>*XYZ Eye Drops*</u> *are covered on all of your patient plans. And the American Academy of Ophthalmology guidelines state that once daily dosing of eye drops is standard of care.*

            So, Doctor, when you prescribe <u>*XYZ Eye Drops*</u>*, you give your patients a fast onset of action, once daily dosing, and an eye drop safe enough for pediatric use. Will you prescribe* <u>*XYZ Eye Drops*</u> *at your next opportunity?*

Doctor: *I can't think of any reason why I wouldn't.*

Rep: *Excellent. How many samples do you think you'll need for the next two weeks?*

Try role-playing different scenarios like the one outlined above. When you're handed one in an interview, you'll be able to breeze right through it. Remember, a one-page detail piece is relatively easy to do. You can find a summary of the main marketing message at the top and near the bottom of the detail piece. If you are given a multi-page detail piece, you'll notice that each page focuses on a different feature and benefit. Look at the last page. There you will find the summary of the main points. Use this to guide you through the entire sales piece.

> ## Secret: Focus On The Abstract When Presenting A Clinical Paper

Another piece of information that a pharmaceutical sales representative uses for selling is a clinical paper. You may be given one to role-play in an interview.

Again, don't panic. You'll go through the same process you went through in presenting the sales aid. You'll be given some time, probably around thirty minutes or so, to read the paper and then come back to the manager and present the clinical paper. As with the detail piece, make sure you ask if they want you to make a sales call or present the clinical paper.

If you've never seen a clinical paper before, and almost no one has before they work in the industry the first place to look is the **Abstract**. (We have an abstract for our fictional <u>*XYZ Eye Drops*</u> in the Appendix of the book.)

The Abstract is located on the front page of the clinical paper and is a summary of the key information and findings that is presented in the clinical paper. At the top of the page is the title of the paper, the authors, the publishers, and other information. Then, the abstract has a summary of the key findings in the clinical paper.

Spend most of your time reading and talking through the Abstract. It summarizes the key points that you need to focus on. Then, read through the entire paper and try to pick out the points in the abstract. This will help you better understand the clinical information. But again, don't worry about trying to thoroughly understand the clinical paper in the short time you have to prepare. You will be trained on all this information when you land the job. The game is to be able to pick out the important points of the clinical paper and present them in a credible manner.

When you go on an interview, take the clinical paper worksheet (in the back of the book) with you in your briefcase. You will likely be given thirty minutes to review the paper before presenting it in the interview. Use the worksheet to help you pull out the pertinent information that you will present to the manager. You'll have time to work out your presentation in private. Generally, while you are working, the manager might make some phone calls, get started on another interview or take a coffee break. Here are the main points to cover in your sales pitch using the abstract.

What to Look for in the Abstract:

- ❖ Title of paper
- ❖ Author(s)
- ❖ Publication (What journal is it published in?)
- ❖ Date
- ❖ Study Design
- ❖ Number of Patients in Study
- ❖ Results
- ❖ Key points (What are the selling points that strengthen the product benefits?)

The exercise below will take you through a practice role-play using a clinical paper covering the key findings in the clinical paper on _XYZ Eye Drops_ in the Appendix of the book.

Exercise: Role-Play Using The Clinical Paper Abstract

Directions: Practice this scenario to get yourself comfortable with presenting a clinical paper using the information in the abstract.

Rep: _Doctor, in the past you've shared your concerns about overprescribing eyes drops for patients to the point of dependency._

Doctor: *That's correct. I prefer they don't use eye drops at all.*

Rep: *I understand. That's why I brought this study to share with you today. Do you have about three minutes for me to walk through the important points?*

Doctor: *Okay, but make it quick.*

Rep: *The title of the study is 'Dry, Itchy Eye: Dependency on Eye Drops,' by John Smith, MD and John Doe, MD. It appeared in the December 2004 issue of the ABC Journal of Medicine.*

It was 21-day, randomized, double-blind, placebo-controlled, multi-center study. There were 345 patients, ages 1-52 years of age with moderate to severe dry, itchy eyes. Patients were randomized to receive one drop per day of <u>XYZ Eye Drops</u> or placebo for 21 days.

The end point measure was patient eye comfort. All patients reported improvement at 48 hours. Thirteen (13) patients continued to need <u>XYZ Eye Drops</u> on an as-needed basis. The remaining patients needed <u>XYZ Eye Drops</u> sporadically based on the season and allergy flare-ups. Only two (2) patients reported a need for continual use.

Doctor: *That's interesting.*

Rep: *Doctor, does this information alleviate your concerns at all?*

Doctor: *Possibly.*

Rep: *Is there any other information you need to see to make you more comfortable prescribing eye drops?*

Doctor: *No, I guess not.*

Rep: *When your patients need relief from dry, itchy eyes, you can feel comfortable prescribing <u>XYZ Eye Drops</u> because it has a fast onset of action, is safe and effective, and has the most convenient dosing available.*

The guidelines of care for dry, itchy eyes state, "once daily eye drops are the standard of care." Doctor, based on the information you've seen in this study, will you prescribe <u>XYZ Eye Drops</u> to your patients with dry itchy eyes?"

Doctor: *Yes. I will.*

Rep: *That's great. How many samples can I leave you today?*

All of the information in the role-play above is clearly spelled out in the clinical paper on _XYZ Eye Drops_ at the back of the book. Present these points and you've hit a home run!

There is also a worksheet in the Appendix for you to use as you break down a clinical paper into a compelling sales message. You can bullet point all the pertinent information from the clinical paper and finish your sales pitch with the marketing message of the product.

Clinical papers are very powerful tools in detailing. Clinical papers provide the scientific results to support and reinforce the messages on the detail piece.

Secret: Practice Presenting A Package Insert (PI)

The PI is the "bible" for a drug. It must be included in every box of samples left with a prescriber.

The PI Covers:

- ❖ The Chemical Structure of the Drug
- ❖ Clinical Pharmacology
- ❖ Pharmacokinetics
- ❖ Indications and Usage
- ❖ Contraindications
- ❖ Warnings
- ❖ Precautions
- ❖ Information for Patients
- ❖ Lab Tests
- ❖ Carcinogenesis, Mutagenesis, and Impairment of Fertility
- ❖ Pregnancy Rating
- ❖ Nursing Mother Precautions
- ❖ Pediatric Use
- ❖ Adverse Reactions
- ❖ Overdosage
- ❖ Dosage and Administration
- ❖ How It is Supplied

The PI lists all the information that was required and approved by the FDA. In short, the PI is the labeling or prescribing information for a drug. The information approved on the PI is the only information a sales representative can provide to prescribers.

The PI is an excellent resource. It is often used in detailing by sales representatives when a prescriber asks questions like, "What does the PI say about visual disturbance with your drug?" "Have you ever heard of anyone getting a rash when using your drug?" You would look in the precautions and adverse events section for this information.

Sometimes a doctor will want to know more about a drug, or have a specific question not addressed in the PI. One thing you can do is send a request to the Drug Information Services department of your company for a literature search to answer these questions for the doctor.

The PI is also used in detailing by sales reps when comparing their drug to a competitor's drug. For example, you might compare the incidence of headache or gastric distress for your drug with a competitor's product. Often the PI has charts showing some of the more common side effects and the incidence of these side effects.

Sometimes prescribers will ask how a side effect of your drug compares with your competitor. You can find out by comparing the PI for both drugs.

Chances are that you will not be asked to present a PI in an interview. It is more common to be asked to present a detail piece or a clinical paper. But, if you're familiar with the PI and how to use it, you'll be impressive.

Secret: Practice Detailing The Way Reps Do It

So, you've been given thirty minutes to review one of these pharmaceutical sales pieces. Now, it's time to go back to the manager and present one of these pieces.

How is it done in the industry? Do I stand or sit? What do I do?

First, you will be sitting, so sit up straight. If you are right handed, hold the detail piece (or clinical paper) in your left hand. Position the piece so that manager can see the page and you can see the page you will be presenting. Hold the detail piece slightly to your left as you would if you were reading a book to a group of children. Hold a pen in your right hand and use that to point to the bolded lines you are reading.

You'll be really impressive if you've been able to memorize some key points during the prep time you've been given in the interview. That way, you can make more eye contact. Point to the chart or graph (if there is one) with the clinical information. Do not use your finger to point. Use a pen. (Be prepared and bring a pen so you don't have to ask to borrow one from the hiring manager!)

You've got to practice this before your interviews because you don't want to come across as a robot as you mechanically try to cover everything. Nor do you want to be clumsy with the detail piece falling down as you try to handle everything. Using a pen can initially feel uncomfortable but over time it becomes natural.

Eye contact is very important for a sales person. So, make sure you break from going over the detail piece to make eye contact with the manager. You should have some movement of your head as you present the detail piece and talk to the manager, too.

It may seem a bit complicated the first couple of times you practice detailing the way seasoned reps do it. But with practice, you'll develop your own detailing style, a style that is natural to you and persuasive to your customers, not only the future prescribers you'll be detailing, but the hiring manager in your interview.

—In A Nutshell—

Learn how to present the classic sales pieces of the pharmaceutical industry:

**The Detail Piece,
The Clinical Paper, and
The PI.**

9

Find The Company And Manager That Is The Right Fit

"To thine own self be true."

—*William Shakespeare*

An important thing to remember during your job quest is to bring your personality and desires into the equation. We've talked a lot about the phases of the process from the pharmaceutical industry's perspective. Companies are trying to find a good fit for them, for the territory where there is an opening, and for the needs and style of the hiring manager.

You need to do your homework, too, on what working at that company would be like. Is the culture right for you? Is the manager's style a good fit for you? You want to make sure you're getting what you bargained for before you accept the offer.

In recruiting you, a company is always putting its best foot forward, just as you are doing yourself. But you want to have a good sense of what the reality of working for that company would be like.

Here's a cautionary tale:

Once upon a time, a successful pharmaceutical sales representative was driving to a sales call. Her car was hit and she got killed. Low and behold, St. Peter met her at the pearly gates. "You're the first sales representative that we've seen up here, so we're not sure what to make of you. We're going to have you spend one day in heaven and one day in hell. Then you can choose where you want to spend eternity."

"Oh, no," said the sales representative, "I'm sure I want heaven." "I'm afraid we have rules," said St. Peter, as he sent her down. The entrance to hell opened and the sales representative stepped onto a lovely town with the streets paved in gold. All her friends from the industry were there. She met the devil, talked to her friends, and had a lovely dinner with fine wine.

The next day, the sales representative spent the day in heaven listening to lutes and angels singing.

When she returned to St Peter, he asked her, "What's your choice?"

The sales rep stopped for a moment, then blurted out, "I'm surprised to say this, but I think I'll take hell. All my friends are there and the place looked great."

She went back down and the entrance to hell opened. She found herself standing in the middle of a desolate, charred terrain with garbage all around. Her friends were there but now they were wearing rags. The devil came up and embraced her.

"I don't get it," said the woman. "Yesterday, everything was so lovely."

The devil grinned, "Yesterday, we were recruiting you. Now, you're staff."

Of course, the fable above is just for fun. But, many candidates who didn't research the company, territory or manager have fallen into job situations that were considerably different from what they expected in the recruiting process.

That's why we think it is always smart to do your own research about companies and cultures though your network of contacts. Always bring questions to each interview that you want to know about the company, its culture, the territory you'll be covering, and what they are looking for in the candidate.

There's a bit of a fine line here. You want to be confident and ask questions, but you don't want to come across as if you think you have the job all wrapped up. Several hiring managers told us that kind of attitude does not go over well.

But you want to be the kind of person who is looking for a good fit for yourself, too. That will make you more appealing, since you'll appear confident. You'll come across as a person with options, not someone desperate for this job.

Secret: Ask The Right Questions At The Right Time

You should always come prepared to ask a few questions. Normally, at the end, an interviewer will ask you if you have any questions. If your response is a deafening silence, you may not come across as on the ball.

A number of managers told us they were turned off by salary questions early in the interview process. Candidates should have an understanding of compensation ranges and use the time for more probing questions. One DM confided that if a candidate asks "How many calls do I have to make per day?" she believes the real question is, "What is the minimal effort I need to expend?" Here's our thought on the way you should approach developing your own questions.

Rules for Candidate Questions:

❖ Keep your questions about the job and its requirements.

❖ Don't bring up salary until the company starts to discuss an offer.

❖ Use questions to gain useful information that will help you frame responses to the interviewer's questions.

❖ Think of the person you are interviewing with and ask appropriate questions.

❖ Consider where you are in the interview cycle.

❖ Always have two to three questions you could ask. When an interviewer asks, "Do you have any questions?" you don't want to greet the question with dead silence.

Phase 1 Questions (To Human Resources, Company Recruiter):

❖ What training does the company provide?

❖ What is the internal promotion policy?

❖ What has been the main reason for people leaving?

❖ What is valued in this company?

❖ What do the communications channels look like? How do they operate?

Phase 2 Questions (To the Hiring Manager, DMs, Group Interviews):

❖ What are the major challenges in this territory?

❖ Why is this position open?

❖ What are my responsibilities as a team member in your sales group?

❖ What are you looking for to complement the current sales group?

❖ How often are performance reviews?

❖ What would you like done differently by the next person in this job?

❖ What are your long-term objectives?

❖ What are some of the difficult challenges facing someone in this job?

❖ What are the critical factors for success in this company?

❖ How would you describe your management style?

❖ How do you like your sales representatives to communicate with you? (Orally, writing, email?)

❖ How is information communicated?

❖ How will you know in six months if you hired the right person?

❖ How does this territory (or drug) affect the company's profit?

❖ What are the most important traits you look for in a sales representative?

Phase 3 Questions (To V.P. Sales and Home Office Executives):

❖ What is the company's mission?

❖ What expansion or changes are planned?

❖ In what ways has this company been the most successful in terms of products?

❖ What significant changes do you see in the near future?

Secret: As The Interview Process Heats Up, Ask For A Ride Along

---

As you progress through the interview process and have become a serious contender for a job offer, a hiring manager may ask you to spend a day in the field with the trainer or a local sales rep (called a ride along in the industry).

If a ride along is not offered, you should request it. (You'll not only look smart and knowledgeable, you'll learn a lot about the job, the territory and the company you might be working for.)

The ride along will give you an up-close look at the day-to-day activity of the job. The ride along gives you the opportunity to see how the company car becomes an office. (The rep escorting you will likely tell you when you get in the car that you're sitting on their desk.) You'll see how the rep packs the trunk, and observe the rep on voice mail and using the laptop. You'll see how the rep plans the call and what samples and literature the rep packs in the bag and how much they pack.

You will have the opportunity to observe how a rep enters an office, quickly sizing up whether or not there is another rep waiting to see the doctor (and how that is handled). You'll learn how to determine how busy the doctor is. This will give you insight into how much time and even *if* the doctor is going to meet with you. The receptionist is called the "gatekeeper." So you'll observe how a rep interacts with that person and the importance of that relationship in the working of the office.

Once the "gatekeeper" waves you back, you'll then get to observe how the rep checks the sample closet and works the other staff and hopefully gains that precious minute or two to speak with the doctor. Throughout the day, you will also observe rejection and how a rep handles that.

There are two very important benefits to the ride along. One, you'll be able to observe the day-to-day activities of the job and think about whether it is right for you. The other benefit is that you'll be able to assess the hiring manager and the company. Feel free to ask lots of job-related questions, including questions about the manager. For example, "What type of manager is Mary?" "What do the reps think are Tom's strengths?"

Be yourself, but remember you are still being interviewed. Making negative comments about your current employer or asking what is the minimum effort required to do the job will be reported back to the manager. (Believe it or not, it happens all the time.) Be friendly with the rep, but not familiar. Do not talk about child-care problems or the myriad of trials you face in your personal life. Everything you do and say will be reported back. In a sense, this your final test. Do not assume at this point you have the job wrapped up. One of the authors spent many days with unsuccessful candidates on their ride alongs. (It's amazing what people will say to you in a car!)

Remember, you are there to observe work in progress. Be professional, friendly, and helpful. Offer to carry some samples, literature and anything else you notice that could help. It will help create a positive impression that could help clinch the job offer. And you'll get valuable information in your trial run about whether you even want the job.

Secret: Find The Right Fit In A Hiring Manager

The person who will have the most impact on your initial career as a sales representative is your hiring manager. So finding someone who has a personality and style that is compatible to yours is crucial.

Here are stories representatives have told us about their hiring manager interviews:

Carol: A Hiring Manager Who Developed A Rookie

I had no sales experience. I'm sure this would not happen today. But, the hiring manager saw something in me that made her think I could be successful. Carol was a wonderful manager for someone as green as me. She left nothing to chance. She showed me how to hold a pen while detailing, how to hold the detail piece, how to connect features to benefits, how to be visual, even how to work the staff. Carol taught me all the basic selling techniques and I became very good at it.

The challenge with Carol was that she wouldn't let go once I become proficient in my skills. This was her management style. Carol was a micromanager. But she was a great manager to work with in my early years. Besides being great at training new recruits, Carol was very good at hiring the right person for a territory. She had a knack for finding the right personality for both rural territories and city territories.

John: A Hiring Manager Who Is A Taskmaster

I had five years sales experience when John hired me. I have tremendous respect for John: he's fair and business-oriented, though definitely not warm and fuzzy. While many reps are intimidated by him, if you do your work and bring in the numbers, he's fine. When a rep gets lazy and sloppy, John is a force to be reckoned with.

John brought my sales skills to the next level. He liked the way I sold, both verbally and visually. John taught me about business entertaining and understanding how to better analyze my territory with the data I was given. He taught me about the numbers game, particularly about how many prescriptions were needed to increase market share on each drug. He emphasized the need for consistency with certain prescibers. John taught me how to determine who gets how much time and energy and the reasons why. John taught me about "front loading" the year with education programs so that you get sales momentum for your drug that helps carry you through the year.

Mike: The Hiring Manager With The Tough Interview Style

The interview was very tough—it was a series of rapid-fire questions. Mike's goal was to learn how I think about business. Do I even understand business? Or would I just go out and drop samples and go home? He grilled me about what I learned from clients after a sales call. "Give me an unexpected opportunity that you capitalized on." "Were you able to keep your customers satisfied without actually saying no?" "Tell me about how you are going to grow your business." "What's on your wish list, and what's on your customer's wish list?"

When I was hired by Mike, he lived up to the promise of the interview. Mike taught me to think big and to think outside the box. Once I had an idea, we would flesh it out so that it fit within all the regulations and rules of the industry. This was a time of great learning and fun.

Mike always related activity to outcomes. "What revenue is that activity going to produce?" "None? Then why bother?" This is when I got interested in the 80/20 principle of evaluating my own efforts. I already knew that 20% of doctors wrote 80% of my business, but I never thought of it in terms of my own activity.

Bill: The Brand New Hiring Manager

Bill had just come right out of the field as a representative, and I was his first rep hire as a hiring manager. Bill had a vision of the talent he wanted in his district. He wanted each individual to bring some different strengths to support team efforts. This served him well when selecting a new candidate. If he had three candidates he liked, he always asked, "With all things being equal, which candidate brings a skill or strength to the team that we don't currently have?" I suppose other managers did this, but I never heard it expressed quite this way. I usually heard who they liked and then it was, "Who do you think would fit the territory best?"

So the interview process is really a two-way process. Of course, the scales are loaded on their side, since in many cases we like the fit and want the job. The best way to get a job offer is to work on your preparation, what you know about the company and the way you present yourself and your accomplishments.

Many pharmaceutical hiring managers, DMs and RMs comment on how nervous so many candidates are during interviews. People expect a certain degree of nervousness, but if you are well prepared, that should be a minimum.

As one hiring manager told us, "If you are too nervous in front of a hiring manager, what will you be like standing in front of a doctor?"

So be prepared. Be confident. And above all, be yourself.

—In A Nutshell—

The process of landing a pharmaceutical rep job is also about finding the right job for you and the right manager for you.

10.

Negotiate The Best Job Offer

"Perseverance is a great element of success.
If you only knock long enough
And loud enough at the gate,
You are sure to wake up somebody."

—*H.W. Longfellow*

How much can I earn? Is the job as lucrative as I've heard? Are there any perks? What can I expect in salary? How do I handle salary questions? How can I get the best offer?

After you go through all the interview rounds, you're practically at the finish line. You may be exhausted from all the rounds of interviews, but you're not there yet until you get a firm offer that is what you want. This chapter will show you how to navigate your way through the final stretch.

Secret: Understand How Compensation Works At The Company As You Negotiate An Offer

---

In the pharmaceutical industry, some companies are open for salary negotiation for people breaking into the business, but most have hard and fast rules concerning what they pay based on your years of experience. You need to find out through networking or through your interviews how the company you are meeting with works.

All companies offer a base salary. The ranges for entry level are $45,000–$55,000, depending on your sales experience and demonstrated sales success. Some companies are open for salary negotiation while others have hard and fast rules as to what they pay based on your years of experience if you are new to the industry.

In addition to a base salary, an incentive is paid based on your sales results. This payout is based on corporate sales goals and could be an additional $25,000–$30,000. Your hiring manager can tell you what the average annual payout of the territory is and you can calculate your total financial package. Of course, you are above average, so you can expect to earn more.

The successful, experienced pharmaceutical sales rep can earn $100,000. The salary packages have changed throughout the years. Some companies ranged from 50% salary plus 50% incentive payout, others offered 60% salary plus 40% incentive payout. The trend today is typically a 70% salary with a 30% incentive payout. But the salary and incentive are only part of the overall package.

The industry thinks in terms of the total compensation package rather than just salary. The base salary is only a small part of the package. It is a good deal: you get a reasonable base pay, an incentive payout based on performance, a company car, profit sharing, pension plan, health insurance and a 401K plan.

The Perks Of A Pharmaceutical Sales Rep:

* ❖ **Company Car.** This is a huge perk! All you do is pick out the color and the car you want from a list of cars. The company's fleet department handles maintenance, insurance and repairs. You will be charged a minimal amount for personal use.

* ❖ **Health Benefits.** Companies offer excellent health benefits at a very reasonable cost to you and your family.

* ❖ **Profit Sharing.** Most of the larger companies offer a 401K profit-sharing plan and some will match a percentage of your savings.

* ❖ **Cell Phone.** Each company policy is different, but some companies will pay a certain amount each month of your cell phone bill for business calls.

* ❖ **Laptop Computer.** Companies will give you a laptop as well as DSL service where it's available. A laptop computer is a must-have tool.

* ❖ **Stock Options.** The stock option plans differ from company to company. This is a great way to build your net worth.

* ❖ **Pension Plan.** Some companies pay out a pension at the time of your retirement at no cost to you. Many plans are a percentage of your salary based on your years of service.

* ❖ **Sales Incentives.** Most companies have extra incentives for top performers. The rewards range anywhere from exotic trips to cars to cash bonuses.

* ❖ **Vacation.** Most companies have a standard three weeks vacation per year. Vacation time increases with your years of service.

As you can see, the total package is impressive. This is indeed a lucrative industry to be a part of. When deciding on which offer to accept, don't just consider the salary package. Consider the entire compensation package.

Secret: Be Aware Of The Background Checks The Company Is Doing

---

So, your resume has been selected, you've been interviewed several times and you feel pretty confident that an offer is coming. There are two other considerations before a manager can offer you the job:

Driving Record
You must have a clean driving record. All companies have a zero tolerance for DUI charges. This is a job killer.

Credit Rating
You should have a good credit rating. After all, you will be responsible for driving and maintaining a company car, managing a territory budget, a credit card and thousands of dollars of product samples.

Whether or not this is a job killer is dependent on each company. We have not heard of anyone being denied a job for this reason, but we can tell you that fiscal responsibility will be an important component of job success.

Secret: Be Savvy About Answering Salary Questions

As you meet with people during the interview process, you'll probably be asked by one or more people, "What salary are you making now?" or "What would it take to bring you on board?" If you are like many candidates, you might think, "Hey, I'm going to get a job offer!" But that isn't necessarily so.

Often salary questions are screening questions. And if you answer it prematurely with a number that is too high, or too low, you could eliminate yourself as a contender. If your salary goals are too high, the hiring manager could think, "Gee, this person won't be happy with the offer we can make." Or, if your number is too low, "Gosh, I thought he'd want more. Must not be as good as he looks." There are some important Do's and Don'ts about handling salary questions during the interview process, but two iron-clad rules.

The Salary Rules:

1. **Don't discuss salary until you have a firm offer.**
2. **Let the company make a specific salary offer first.**

The way to play the game when you are asked these questions is to parry the salary question back to the interviewer. In early stage interviews, say something like, "I think it is premature to discuss salary at this point. We can readdress salary when we both feel that I could make an important contribution to the sales team." Or, "I would prefer to learn more about the position first before we discuss salary."

If you are asked in an application to state your salary requirements, leave the line blank, or write in "Open." Do not write in your salary history in applications or cover letters, either. If you match the job specs, you will not be screened out by most companies. If you feel you must include your salary history, be sure to include total compensation.

In later interviews, your hiring manager will most likely bring up the salary question. The best way to answer is to say something like, "Your company is known for a fair compensation scale, and if we decide that I'm a good fit for your sales team, I am sure we will be able to agree on a salary base."

Or you could say, "I want to learn more about the opportunity in the territory and at ABC Company first, but I am sure salary won't be a problem." An alternative is, "The key question is what you have budgeted for the base salary. What is the range for the job?" When the hiring manager gives you a number, you can respond in several ways. You could follow up with, "That is more conservative than I would have expected. How flexible is that dollar amount?"

Remember, as a rookie pharmaceutical sales representative, you won't have a lot of flexibility in your base salary. Once you get to specialty sales, negotiating base salary is more common. A sales rep we know named Meg just changed companies and went into specialty sales. She requested an additional $10,000 in her base and one more week of vacation. Meg took a risk in asking for the jump she did, but she got it. They really wanted her. So, they came back and said, "Yes, when can you start?"

Secret: Know How To Handle The Offer

When you are made an offer, you have three ways to act. You can accept on the spot. You can thank them for the offer and ask for some time to evaluate it and get back to them. You can haggle by asking if there is some flexibility to the offer. (Presumably, you wouldn't have stayed in the running if you were going to turn them down flat. But even if you plan to reject the offer, ask for time to think it over and come back to them.)

The best course, in our view, is option two. You should never try to negotiate at the time you receive an offer. If you think the offer can be improved upon, it is much more effective to come back after a couple of days after you have determined your goals and had time to discuss the offer with someone who understands the business.

With time, you can determine trade-offs and your walk-away point. The way to get a sweeter deal is to tell them the truth. You can call the hiring manager, and say something like, "I've been able to evaluate the offer and I'm excited about the contributions I can make to your sales team. I think it's a very good fit. There are a couple of areas I would like to talk about, and once these are resolved, I am ready to start." Then you should go over the areas of agreement, focus on what you can accomplish in the territory based on your past record, then address the items you want the hiring manager to consider, usually the base salary.

As we have told you, there is not a lot of flexibility for a rookie sales representative. Pharmaceutical companies need to keep the offer in a competitive range with other new representatives. If there is a big discrepancy, you probably have not done your homework well in terms of base salary available for someone with your experience. However, you may be able to get a salary improvement to the high end of the range depending on how much the manager wants you.

Above all, be confident, but empathetic. What you want is a win—win. You want to get the compensation you want. And the company wants to feel it recruited a talented sales representative at competitive terms.

After all, this is just the beginning of your new career as a pharmaceutical sales rep. And these are the people you'll be meeting again and again as you interview for your next promotion.

—In A Nutshell—

Your perseverance has paid off.
You made the final round.
Be savvy about how to negotiate the offer.

11.

Get Off To A Good Start: Training, Samples, And Your Territory

"The beginning is the most important part of the work."

—*Plato*

About a week after you've finished all the new hire paperwork, you'll be hit by a blizzard. You will receive a mountain of learning modules on just about everything. This is your first taste of training, pharmaceutical sales rep style. As you will soon find out, training is an ongoing part of the sales rep job. It starts as soon as you accept the job offer.

Here's a short list of the information that will be sent to your home:

- ❖ Company Policies
- ❖ Compliance Issues
- ❖ Fraud and Abuse Policies
- ❖ Job Expectations
- ❖ Laptop Instructions
- ❖ Anatomy and Physiology Training Modules
- ❖ Disease State Training Modules
- ❖ Specific Drug Sales Aids and Information

All this information can be overwhelming and intimidating. It's probably the first time you've ever seen, or paid attention to, words like "pharmacokinetics" or "pharmacodynamics." Don't worry. You'll be able to learn it. It seems as if you need to know everything, and you're right. The expression many managers and home office people use most often is "You need to know this inside and out, backwards and forwards."

Secret: Take The Home Study Seriously And Bond With Your Trainer

The person you need to bond with during this first home-study phase is your trainer. You'll get two weeks to one month of home study when you start out. Your trainer will be your lifeline. The trainer will direct your overall schedule of study. The trainer will supervise you as you read and complete assessments through the entire home study period. Your trainer is there for any and all questions. So, ask them! Don't be afraid to ask questions to make sure you understand what you are reading.

As the time nears for your home office training, you will likely spend more time with your trainer talking through the material that you have read. You need to be able to demonstrate that you understand the information before going to home office. Often you will take a mastery test that is facilitated by your trainer and then faxed to home office for grading. You will be expected to get a high grade, about 95%, on your mastery tests before you can go to home office. This is not like college, where getting a minimal passing mark is acceptable. Some companies may expect you to score as high as 99%.

Secret: Be Prepared For A Rigorous Home Office Training

Once you have successfully completed the home study part of training, it's off to your company's home office for initial training.

Most reps report that home office training is very intense and competitive. Depending on the products you're selling, you may be at home office training for two to four weeks and sometimes longer. If your company has over three weeks of in-house training, you will likely be able to go home on some weekends, or maybe your family can come to visit you. It all depends on company policy.

The training is conducted in a classroom setting and you will have lectures from many home office people such as product mangers, the VP of Sales, and representatives from HR, Sample Accountability and Drug Information Services. Here you'll meet other new reps from across the country and may create lasting friendships. It is good to bond with at least one person as you can share with each other the challenges you are facing with the new job.

While training is conducted in a classroom setting, you are expected to already know the information. Home Office training is to reinforce and further explain what you already learned in home study.

Remember your college days when you were spoon-fed information? This is nothing like that. You should be well prepared when you arrive. You will be asked a lot of questions. It will be very obvious if you are not prepared, and this is reported back to your trainer and manager. Reps have been sent home from home office training. You won't look like a good hire and your trainer and manager won't look good either.

You will be tested several times throughout the training. Many companies test your product knowledge that first morning. This is before any lectures or opportunity for questions. These tests are scored and your scores are reported to you, your trainer and manager by the following day. After this first test, the lectures will begin. Then, there will be more tests, and eventually you will begin role-play.

At the end of your home office training, a performance evaluation will be written and sent to your trainer and manager. Some of the things written up include your overall performance in class—level of participation, product knowledge, respect toward speakers and classmates and negative comments. Even your evening activities will be reported back to your hiring manager. So, watch your P's and Q's, whether it's too much drinking, not participating in group homework assignments, or lateness in the mornings when meeting the van to take you and your classmates from the hotel to the home office.

Secret: Role-Play And Training Are The Way Of Life In The Pharmaceutical Industry

---

Role-play is an integral part of the career of a pharmaceutical sales rep. Throughout your career, there will be constant role-play, when new detail pieces are introduced, at meetings to launch new drugs, and when new clinical papers have been approved for detailing. You will role-play whenever anything new is rolled out in the marketplace for promotional use.

Once you complete your initial training at the home office, you go back home and prepare to go out into your territory with your trainer for the first few days. Then, you'll likely work by yourself for a few weeks and your manager will then work with you.

After about six months working in your territory, it is time to go back to home office for advanced training. This training can be anywhere from one to three weeks and most reps report feeling more confident at this point. Training doesn't feel as intense as it did in initial training.

You may be asked to bring an assignment to demonstrate your business knowledge of your territory. You will role-play to fine-tune your skills and to become more comfortable using clinical studies when selling.

When you have completed advanced training, you will go back to your territory and continue contact with your trainer. You will receive ongoing coaching and training from your manager as a matter of business practice in the industry.

So, now you have completed your start up training and you are expected to grow the business in your territory. But training doesn't end here. Ask any rep and they'll probably tell you they feel like they spend half of their time at night completing some training.

There is a lot of online training. On a regular basis, you'll have compliance guidelines as well as fraud and abuse guidelines. You'll also access online information on new indications for products you are currently selling, new product launches, and new computer programs. You can access on-line instruction about sample accountability, expense reports or any new system or change the company implements that requires new knowledge or skills.

Training is also done at district meetings, regional meetings and national meetings. Training is a fact of life in this industry. You need a mindset that is open to learning new information on a regular basis and learning it quickly.

Secret: Samples, Samples And More Samples

One responsibility of the job that can keep a rep awake at night is samples. Among those mountains of boxes that arrive soon after you have accepted the job offer will be lots of product samples.

It is very important that you open every box and take inventory of everything. You will be held accountable for the samples you receive. Check each box against the packing slip so you can verify that you received what the home office says they sent you. You should inventory every box of each product sample: the size of the box, the number of tablets or devices in each box. There are often different sizes and strengths of each product you sell and you have to keep track of each separately. Different sizes, strengths or numbers of pills in a box are color-coded. So make sure each size and color matches with the packing slip inside the box.

You are expected to sign a receipt and then return the packing slip with your signature to an address at the home office shown on the packing slip. Once you have signed for the samples, unless you state otherwise, you are accountable for the numbers on that packing slip.

Sales reps keep their samples and literature in either a rented storage unit or their home or garage. Most companies will reimburse you if you use a storage unit and it certainly separates the job from you a bit. The downside of the storage unit is that you have to meet the delivery person at the unit to accept samples and literature and go there every morning or evening to pack your car.

Storing your samples and literature in your garage or a room in your house is certainly more convenient. You can schedule early morning deliveries before going out for the day or late deliveries at the end of your workday. Everything you need to pack is right there at your fingertips. The downside of keeping things at home is that the samples can literally take over your house.

Secret: Take An Inventory Of Your Samples At The End Of The Month

---

You are accountable for the number of samples you leave in each office. A physician will sign for receipt of the samples you leave and then you deduct this number from your inventory. It's a little bit like keeping a checkbook. Samples received are added to your balance. Samples left in a doctor's office are deducted from your balance.

Several times throughout the year, you have to reconcile your balance with what the home office balance shows. Sounds easy, right? You can add and subtract, no problem.

Yes, but many a successful rep has been kept awake at night because the actual samples one has in their possession does not reconcile with what home office says you should have.

How does this happen? It's a little like that missing sock that never makes it out of the dryer. We haven't talked to a rep who could explain this, except sometimes you get so busy talking in the doctor's office, you leave two boxes of samples and mark that on the signature card or laptop and as you're walking out you get a request for three more boxes. You are so sure you'll remember so you go to the car, get three more boxes and drop them off in the office. You talk some more, go back to the car, write some post call notes and you're off to the next call. Those three boxes just left your mind, and so it goes.

You will need to take inventory yourself at the end of every month just for your own information. At different times throughout the year you will be notified by the Sample Accountability Department that they are sending you an inventory worksheet for you to fill out and return. You will count your samples, fill in the worksheet and return it to home office. Then, several times per year, a contractor that your company hires will call you to set up an appointment with you to come to your home or storage unit to count your sample inventory.

If you don't take inventory yourself, by the time a formal inventory is taken you can be missing cases of samples. Yes, cases. One author has spent many nights talking to rep colleagues about this very issue—"What am I going to do?" Most companies allow a small variance of how many sample boxes can go unaccounted for, but it is not many and this can be a job killer. Companies are responsible for reporting their sampling activity to the FDA and are accountable for the thousands of reps they hire. Individual rep names are reported to the FDA. When that happens, someone from the agency will probably come to your storage unit or home to count. As you can imagine, it's a very nerve-wracking experience and one you want to avoid at all costs.

Secret: Be Prepared For Territory Realignment

When you are hired, you are accepting a position for a specific territory—Mainville, USA and outlying suburbs. This is a perfect fit for where you live. This is where you are going to work for the life of your career with Company A, right?

Wrong! If you stay with one company for several years, your territory will change many times based on realignments.

What is a realignment?

A realignment is the reconfiguring of territories usually done nationwide to meet company objectives. Realignments occur because of shifts in the sales force or a merger that includes drugs with different disease states. They are also done when there is a need to refocus the target audience or a new product launch.

Realignments are usually done by an outside contractor. All the relevant information, such as target audience, zip codes and number of reps (including you) is fed into a computer. Out come the new territories. Often, a rep will find that he or she has different zip codes and sometimes even a whole new territory. As with all changes in business responsibility, some people are undisturbed, some people are happy, and some are very unhappy.

Marlene's Story

I was an experienced sales rep and accepted a position with a prestigious pharmaceutical company as a specialty rep. It was the perfect territory. And the first time I had ever lived inside my territory. So now I didn't have to drive 45 miles to get to my territory—I woke up in it.

When I took over the territory, it was ranked 119th out of 120 in the nation. Within six months, I grew the business so it ranked 2nd out of 120 in the nation. Set for life in this new territory, one might think, no?

Of course not. Right before the holiday break, I was told that with the realignment I was being moved to a territory that was 25 miles from where I lived. Now the closest point for me is 25 miles away. Needless to say, I was very unhappy about this turn of events. Most importantly, the territory that I worked so hard in and had turned completely around was being given to another rep.

Though I'm sure I'm not the first rep with this experience, it still was a bitter pill to swallow. I spoke to my manager, but was told that the realignment was set in stone and would happen after the New Year.

When this happens to you, you can move on and accept the new territory, or, if you can't get past the situation, you'll have to start your job hunt again.

The moral of my story is that you have to be flexible in this industry or you have to move on. I'm moving on.

Realignments are a fact of life in the industry and you will be confronted with it again. Maybe, next time you'll be the recipient of a high performing territory. This high performing territory is now yours to maintain and grow. Many reps like inheriting a low performing territory. Those reps have a positive outlook and say "There's nowhere to go but up."

> ## Secret: Be Effective With Your Target Audience: Doctors And Healthcare Professionals

A lot is written about the different personalities of doctors. Some approaches even try to fit all doctors into one of a handful of personality types.

The bottom line is doctors are people first with a myriad of personalities just like the rest of us. And, like us, they have families, outside interests and other things that play on their minds during the day. Just as we may be shy or aggressive (and a myriad of variations in between), so are they. While trying to figure out which personality type a doctor is can be helpful, most reps report that it is hard to do. On a sales call, you have to be able to respond in the moment. And, you're only getting a snapshot of who the person is in a short sales call.

As a sales professional, your interpersonal skills should be fairly good and you should be able to adjust your style to meet the style and temperament of your customer. It's not that you're trying to be someone you aren't, but rather to be appropriate in different situations. For example, you wouldn't likely behave the same way at your child's soccer game as you would while having tea with the Queen of England. Different situations require that we present different facets of ourselves at the appropriate times.

After interviewing many seasoned sales reps and managers, the doctor "types" were simplified as:

Some doctors are satisfied with the marketing message.

Others want the science and clinical information that justify the marketing message.

Like any sales situation, the approach you take *depends* on the situation at hand. It depends on how new the product and information is, it depends on how rushed the doctor is at that moment, it depends on how well you presented the sales pitch, it depends on what other challenges the doctor has going on at that moment.

It depends. As a sales professional, it is your responsibility to read the situation and deliver the information the best way the doctor will receive it at that moment, during that call, that day. You will be calling on the same doctor again and will have other opportunities to deliver your information.

Having said that, physicians we interviewed shared some similar expectations that they all have of sales reps:

❖ Be efficient—come with a plan and bring intellectual value such as a new finding on the science behind the drug.

❖ Schedule appointments when it is convenient for the doctor to spend time with you, even if the office policy is a drop-in. Many physicians we interviewed said they would be willing to sit down and spend time with a rep, but reps don't ask for it.

❖ Be knowledgeable—know your product, disease state, current impending problems, lay press and the latest journals.

❖ Be resourceful—know how to save patients money, to get requested information quickly, and to be aware of resources outside of your company (such as patient education programs at the local hospital).

❖ Be personable—present balanced information, do not manipulate, become part of the office team.

Secret: Plan Your Career Path

Be prepared to put in long hours at first, but also think about where you want to be headed in the industry. The most common next steps are becoming a specialty rep, a hospital rep or a trainer. Here's a snapshot of these jobs.

The Specialty Representative

A specialty rep is a promotion from the primary care marketplace. Many managers require over five years of experience selling to primary care physicians as a basic requirement to applying for a specialty job. If you enjoy your rep job, this is definitely something to strive for.

A specialty rep must be very knowledgeable about the disease state, product, and target audience. Often, a specialty rep only calls on one specialty, such as cardiologists or oncologists.

There are a lot of advantages to this job over the primary care sales rep job. First, you'll be competing with fewer other specialty reps for a doctor's time. So, gaining access can be a little easier (although it's never easy). Specialists know that you are a seasoned rep and understand that this is a promotion. You'll find that many doctors will respect your knowledge and experience. Your skills are polished, you have more experience and are able to converse with them on a different level.

Specialty reps are more clinical and have more opportunities to share clinical information. Specialists are not as interested in the marketing message and sales aid as they are in studies and clinical papers. Specialists tend to want to see the scientific proof of what you tell them about your drug. The bottom line is, as a specialty rep you need to be very comfortable in explaining science.

The Hospital Representative

The hospital rep position is a promotion from either the primary care sales force or the specialty sales force. This job usually requires five years of successful sales experience. As a hospital rep, your territory will be teaching hospitals and large community hospitals with over 300 beds. The hospital rep may be part of a district, but the larger companies generally have a hospital division with separate management.

Hospital reps call on staff (also called attending) physicians, fellows and residents in the areas relating to the drugs they are selling. For example, a hospital rep selling a product for cardiovascular diseases would call on the cardiology attending physicians, fellows and residents who are working their cardiology rotation. Hospital reps educate the residents on the drugs they sell, which ones are on formulary (the recommended list of the hospital) and which ones are being considered for formulary status.

Hospital reps also call on the hospital pharmacy. The most important person in the pharmacy is the PharmD or clinical pharmacist, although the Director of Pharmacy and buyer are also important customers.

One of the responsibilities of the hospital rep is to get their product on the hospital formulary. This requires meeting with the pharmacists and discussing the clinical and scientific benefits of the drug. The pharmacist must have a thorough understanding of the drug and be convinced there is a patient benefit to having the drug available for physicians to prescribe. Hospital pharmacists determine whether or not the benefits warrant the cost of the drug to the hospital. Physicians must also want to have access to the drug. The pharmacist takes the information to the Pharmacy and Therapeutics Committee (P&T Committee) which meets several times a year to present the drug and its benefits. The P&T Committee will approve or disapprove adding the drug to the formulary.

If the drug does not receive approval, the job is not done. The hospital rep then has to solicit more advocates from physicians who want to have the drug available for their patients. If the drug is added to the hospital formulary, it is the hospital rep's responsibility to get physicians to prescribe the drug. Like any product, a hospital rep must pull through the business.

The Trainer

There is a constant flow of new information, new drugs, new studies, and new regulations that all reps need to stay abreast of, so training is part and parcel of life as a pharmaceutical sales rep. The trainer is responsible for training new hires as well as coaching peers on just about everything taking place.

The trainer teaches sales reps everything from new industry information to product knowledge and detail aids, to sharing best practices and everything in between. You name it, and there is probably a training module on it. Your trainer is your "go-to person" to help you become effective in your job and getting up to speed in your territory as quickly as possible.

In some companies, the trainer is an additional assignment for a sales rep who is selected within a district, called a district trainer. In other companies there are regional trainers that are designated to train new hires and other training assignments within a specified region. The regional trainer position is a developmental position for sales reps who want to become district managers.

Reps who are interested in becoming a district sales trainer can apply directly to their manager. The district trainer is responsible for helping anyone who needs assistance. In addition to training, the trainer must maintain their own territory business as a rep and all associated responsibilities. The trainer is a rotational position lasting one year, although it is not uncommon for a trainer to retain the position because they are particularly good at it.

The regional trainer position is a new job that was established to gain consistency in field training. Before, each district would have different trainers. Now, with a regional trainer, there is one trainer for many districts. Plus, the regional trainer is not distracted by rep responsibilities and is totally focused on training.

The regional trainer travels in the assigned region training new hires across many districts and reporting to many different managers. Since regional trainers do not have a territory to manage, they attend district meetings where they might hold mini training sessions on a new sales aid. They also might work in the field with a rep.

The regional trainer position is intended to be a stepping-stone for a rep who wants to become a district manager.

Secret: Learn How To Handle Doctor Rejection

Rejection on any level is tough for all of us, but as a new pharmaceutical sales rep, it feels like the end of the world.

You may not want to admit it, but if you're like lot of new reps, asking to talk to a doctor can be intimidating. After all, you're used to being a patient and viewing the doctor as the expert. Now, the roles are reversed in a way. You are presenting yourself as an expert on your drug and therapy area to doctors. It is a daunting task the first few times you put yourself in that position.

As a sales rep, there are layers of rejection that you need to learn how to handle. The first type of rejection is by the receptionists—the office gatekeepers—who won't even give you an opportunity to let the doctor reject you. You walk into the waiting room, up to the check-in counter, and ask to see the doctor. The receptionist may not even look up from her work as she says, "No, he's too busy," or "No, he's seen too many reps today."

What do you do? You thought you were going to be welcomed with open arms, right? No, you're new. You have to earn that. So, now what do you do? Well, you need to ask what the office policy is for seeing the doctor. If you come back, will the receptionist help you get in to see the doctor? Give her some power and let her know that you know she holds the key for your success.

So now you've made it through the gatekeeper to see the doctor. You're a bit nervous but if you talk about what you know, the doctor won't ask questions and you'll live to tell about it. What happens, though, when you don't convey the information well? You start to talk to the doctor and the doctor tells you flatly, "I don't want to listen to you today." Or, "I don't like this lunch you brought." Or, "I'm tired of all you reps lying to me." Or, "Don't come back until you have something new to tell me."

The rejection can be brutal and is often forthright. What do you do? You nurse your ego. You call a rep friend and commiserate. You pick yourself up and go on to the next call. It is usually not personal, although pay attention to the comments. Maybe you're not bringing new information. Maybe, at that moment, the doctor is pressed for time and you are one more person who wants something. Maybe next time you need to observe better what is going on in the office. Maybe you should ask if you could schedule an appointment at a more convenient time. There are always things you can do to try to minimize the rejection, but it will never go away completely.

Rejection is a part of sales. It's tough, but you have to be tougher. Stay positive and always be pleasant. The next time you call on the doctor the previous interaction will likely be forgotten.

—In A Nutshell—

Be prepared for long hours in the beginning.
You will be trained and trained.
And you'll be hit with a deluge of samples and product information.

12.

Sell Smart To Succeed In This Dynamic And Competitive Industry

"If you don't change, you're going to like irrelevance even less."
—*General Eric Shinseki,* former Chief of Staff, U.S. Army

As a pharmaceutical sales representative, you will have to operate in a world of wall-to-wall information and demands. Today, you are not just hired to do a job, you are hired to think and do the job more efficiently and more effectively. With the internet at our disposal, we all have access to the same information. We have the same number of hours in a day and we all have numerous competitors.

So, if your job is to beat the competition, how do you do that in today's marketplace?

You need to be first in the mind of the doctors in your territory. You need to be first in providing the best clinical information on your drug, you need to be first in capturing mindshare, you need to be first in adding value, you need to be first in getting a reaction, and you need to be first in valuing your customer's time.

Today there are more limitations on the sales rep/physician relationship under all the new regulations and guidelines such as HIPAA, PhRMA and OIG. So, more than ever before, you need to become the kind of person the doctor and the other staff in the office want to make time for.

Secret: You Need To Sell SMART

We developed a new approach to sales called Sell SMART™. This approach offers something for all stakeholders, including you! Once you are respected for the value you bring to the table, your job will be more fulfilling, in both increased income and increased job satisfaction.

Let's look at what SMART means and how that fits with your job as a pharmaceutical sales rep.

S   —   Sell **Science**
M   —   Capture **Mindshare**
A   —   Become the **Added Value**
R   —   Get a **Reaction**
T   —   Leave **Triggers** and Footprints

Secret: Uncover The Science Behind Your Drug

Don't just focus only on the product benefits. While it has its place, we believe it is the old way of selling. If you want to be a top sales rep, you must bring *intellectual value* to doctors and health care providers. That's why we think it is important to present the science behind a drug. When you bring new information, you'll have a much greater chance of becoming the type of sales rep that healthcare providers want to see.

Of course, you must promote the drug based on the approved indications. However, you will often have to get prescribers to think differently about your drug. Give the prescriber better clinical reasons to prescribe your product over its competitors. Uncover the challenge within the disease state or therapy class.

Example: Role-Play For Selling The Science Behind Your Drug

Directions: In this scenario, you are selling to a doctor who has been prescribing your biggest competitor. The doctor has just told you that patients have been having trouble with the dosing schedule, and there is a high incidence of non-compliance.

Doctor: *All the eye drops are the same in terms of efficacy. Patients just need to use them.*

Rep: *You're right, doctor. Patients do need to use their medication correctly to get the desired results. As you know, a dosing schedule plays a very important role in compliance. XYZ Eye Drops are the only eye drops that offer once daily dosing, plus our studies demonstrate patients experience relief of dry eye within 48 hours.*

Doctor: *Mmm. I didn't realize XYZ Eye Drops had a once a day dosing schedule. That would probably help a lot of my patients, but what about efficacy? Isn't it better to use eye drops frequently to keep the eyes moistened?*

Rep: *The number of drops used does not necessarily correlate to efficacy and if your patients aren't compliant they are not likely to get the relief they need for their dry, itchy eyes.*

Our study that appeared in ABC Medical Journal demonstrated efficacy at 48 hours.

Doctor: *Oh, how many patients were in the study?*

Rep: *There were 345 patients, ages 1-52 years of age with moderate to severe dry, itchy eyes. It was a 21-day, randomized, double-blind, placebo-controlled, multi-center study. The end point measure was patient eye comfort. All patients reported improvement at 48 hours.*

Doctor: *Interesting. I'll give XYZ a try.*

Rep: *Great. I think your patients will appreciate the fast onset of action and the convenient dosing schedule of XYZ Eye Drops. How many samples should I leave today?*

How can you provide the science behind a drug? Well, how knowledgeable are you? Knowledge is intellectual value. For example, look at the following areas.

❖ Are you well read? Do you keep up with all the clinical information your company sends you? Do you read journals and industry news?

❖ Do you know what resources are available from your company?

❖ Are you up-to-date on your drug and others in its therapy class?

Secret: Find Ways To Capture Mindshare For Yourself And Your Drug

---

Mindshare. What is it?

Mindshare is an important marketing and media concept originally developed by the advertising industry. In a highly competitive marketplace with many competing messages, the winning brand is the one that captures the minds of prospects more than competing products.

Marketers and advertisers measure mindshare, such as which brand is top-of-mind or consistently said first when asked about that brand category. And they rank all brands in a category in terms of mindshare in research done with consumers. Mindshare is important because research shows that people favor brands (or anything really) that is top-of-mind or has strong mindshare. They buy them more, and recommend them to friends.

It's the same way with you and your drug. You want to build mindshare with the prescribers in your territory for you as a sales rep and for the drug you are selling. Once you begin to provide a higher level of science to show the clinical benefit of your drug over its competitors, you will capture their mindshare. That is, when a prescriber has a particular challenge, they will seek you out. You want to be the rep your docs want to see. Let the doors close to everyone else.

There are other ways to build mindshare as well. For example, today, health care is high profile. It is constantly in the news. (Good and bad sides to that as far as the pharmaceutical industry is concerned.) What are the doctor's patients reading or hearing in the news? Will this information affect the doctor? How? Is there a report or information from your home office that you could provide that will help clarify the issue? Are you well networked? Is there something going on in the community that your prescribers would want to know about?

The goal is to get the doctor to seek you out for any challenge, any reason to give you the opportunity to detail the clinical benefits of your drug. You want to be the rep that is top-of-mind with the doctors in your territory.

Secret: Become The Added Value

Too often doctors feel that sales reps are a waste of time. Doctors have told us that reps just focus on selling the benefits of their drug. Most doctors feel they already know that, and that they want something more. That's why you have to become the added value.

You are valued because you bring value. You bring products and relevant clinical information that helps health care providers and they recognize it.

Your company and community have a lot of resources that can help you become the added value in your territory. Use them and make them available to help position yourself as the go-to person in that disease state. Community hospitals provide patient education programs in the evenings for a variety of health related issues. Are you aware of them?

There are lots of ways you can provide added value for your prescribers. Are you aware of the resources available for patients in the community? It is very helpful to doctors if you know what's going on in the community and what their colleagues are doing.

For example, if you sell a drug for asthma, maybe you can provide information on community services to the prescribers in your territory. Asthma patients need a lot of education and training on how to use inhalers. One-time instruction in the doctor's office is usually not enough. Do you know about workshops at community hospitals that provide educational programs? Where are they? What time? What is the phone number to get more information? Do you need a reservation?

Most community hospitals put out monthly or quarterly bulletins that list all the support groups and educational programs. Are you on the mailing list? If you are, it's another way to provide information to the doctors in your territory. Here's an exercise to get you started.

Exercise: Become The Go-To Person For Prescribers

Directions: Compile a list of resources and programs that might be helpful to the health care providers in your territory.

Community Programs

_____

_____

_____

Hospital Programs

_____

_____

_____

Local Colleges

_____

_____

_____

Secret: Think Of The Reaction You Want From The Prescriber, And What You Need To Do To Get That Reaction

---

Before each sales call, think of the most impactful way to present the sales message to that specific prescriber. Develop your sales call presentation based on the result you want to achieve. Don't think of what you want to say. Rather, ask yourself, what do they want to hear? What *reaction* do you want from the individual you will be seeing? What do you need to do to get that reaction?

So, you're probably thinking, that's easy to answer. I want them to write more prescriptions for my drug. Of course, that is the end result you want. But to get that reaction, you will have to have different approaches based on the needs and inclinations of particular prescribers. Is this the doctor who is satisfied with the marketing message? Is this the doctor who wants to discuss the clinical paper?

For the doctors in your territory, you'll need to ask and answer some questions:

❖ Do I give them reasons to want and need to see me?

❖ Do I bring more intellectual value and substance to the interaction than my competitor?

❖ Do my prescribers' eyes glaze over when I speak, or do I get a reaction from them?

❖ Can I see in their expression or through what they tell me that I've given them something to think about?

❖ Have I challenged their thinking or prescribing habits in any way?

❖ Are they listening to me? Or am I so expected, they don't need to listen anymore. They just have their pen in hand ready to sign for samples.

❖ If prescribers described the ideal rep, do I have any of those characteristics and behaviors? Can I develop them?

Create reasons why a prescriber would want and need to really listen to you. Give them clinical information to think about and to move the conversation forward.

Providing science, capturing mindshare and adding value will differentiate you from other reps and increase your business stature with your prescribers. Think about what resources you can provide that prescribers want and need. Here's an exercise to help you come up with innovative ways to be relevant to prescribers.

Exercise: Getting The Right Reaction

Directions: One way to come up with new sales approaches is to turn the situation around. Put yourself in the doctor's shoes, and answer these questions:

Would you be challenged if a sales rep used the exact same approach? Explain why or why not.

_____

_____

How would you react? Would you want to listen?

_____

_____

Is there a reason to see the sales rep again? Are they bringing relevant clinical information?

_____

_____

What would be a more effective approach to get the reaction you want?

_____

_____

Secret: Leave Triggers And Footprints

Time is limited. Doctors (like all of us) are busier than ever. Why spend it with a rep that offers nothing other than samples?

Time and time again, here are the complaints physicians brought up about reps in our interviews:

* ❖ Lack of preparation
* ❖ No real reason for asking for their time other than getting a signature for samples
* ❖ Same old message they told me on the last sales call

Use your doctor's time wisely and make the most of the time spent with them. Human beings by nature want to be stimulated by ideas and information they find useful or interesting. One way to do that is by leaving triggers and footprints.

Triggers are marketing materials and clinical information provided to you by your company to leave behind with prescribers. When placed strategically, i.e. prescriber's office, the lab, or near the sample closet, they act as reminders of your product or discussion. Triggers act to extend the life of your message. Remember, you want your product to be top of mind!

Footprints are anything that has your contact information on it, i.e. your business card. You should always leave footprints so that when your prescribers need to contact you, they have easy access to your information. Remember, you want to be top of mind and easy to reach when needed!

Use your time wisely as well. While you need to cover the bases with all the prescribers in your territory, focus on prescribers who can impact your business the most. Plan your day. Plan your calls. When your sales approach isn't working, look for a better way. We can't change other people's behavior, but we can change our own. When we change our approach, it requires the other person to respond differently.

Since one of the authors carried the bag for fourteen years, we know there will always be the thirty-second feature/benefit call for a sales rep. But, prescribers are busier now than ever before. There are more reps than ever before. The more you provide science and bring intellectual value to your prescribers, the more reason you give them to spend time with you.

Develop a plan to sell "SMART" in your territory. It will give you a lot of advantages. Selling smart compels you to think, and that in itself will start to give you an advantage over many people. Selling smart also compels you to think big picture and long term, rather than small picture and short term. Sell SMART will help you build a dynamic career as a pharmaceutical sales representative.

—In A Nutshell—

Sell SMART:

S — Sell **Science**

M — Capture **Mindshare**

A — Become the **Added Value**

R — Get a **Reaction**

T — Leave **Triggers** and Footprints

Secrets' Sample Selling Tools

Sample Detail Piece

This is a fictional drug detail piece for teaching purposes only. Any information that reflects a marketed product is coincidental.

FOR A QUICK RESPONSE TO DRY, ITCHY EYES, THINK *XYZ EYE DROPS* FIRST

XYZ Eye Drops – Once a Day for Dry, Itchy Eyes

	XYZ Eye Drops	Competitor A	Competitor B
Dosing	1 drop/day	5 drops/day	4 drops/day
Relief in 48 Hours	Yes	No	No
Pediatric Use	Yes	No	No

XYZ Eye Drops: Fast, Safe, Effective Relief From Dry, Itchy Eyes
XYZ Eye Drops provide the greatest improvement in dry, itchy eyes within the first 48 hours of treatment.
In a 21-day, well-controlled clinical trial, 345 patients with dry, itchy eyes were treated with *XYZ Eye Drops*. At 48 hours, there was a 98% improvement in the primary symptoms of dry, itchy eyes in the drug treatment group versus placebo.
Please see full prescribing information.
References: Smith, Doe Drug Information Report, December, 2004

Eye Lubricant   For fast response *XYZ Eye Drops*

Sample Clinical Paper Abstract

This is a fictional clinical paper abstract for teaching purposes only. Any information that reflects a marketed product is coincidental.

ABC JOURNAL OF MEDICINE

Published at www.xxx.org December, 2004

DRY, ITCHY EYE: DEPENDENCY ON EYE DROPS

John Smith, MD, Steve Doe. MD

ABSTRACT Increased need for eye moisturizing has been reported in patients with dry, itchy eyes. Initial reports indicate that when eye moisturizers are used the normal tearing process may be interrupted. Eye Lubricant is a synthetic solution for optical use only. Dry eye is a common problem for patients with and without allergies.

In this case report, 345 patients (aged 1–52 years) with dry, itchy eyes were evaluated as of December 2000. At that time, patients received 1 drop in each eye daily of Eye Lubricant or placebo for 21 days.

Eye Lubricant drops were discontinued after 21 days. Thirteen (13) patients continued to need Eye Lubricant on an as needed basis. The remaining patients needed Eye Lubricant sporadically based on the season and during allergy flare-ups. Only two (2) patients reported a need for continual use.

Study Objective: To evaluate the ongoing need for Eye Lubricant in the treatment of dry, itchy eyes.
Design: A 21-day, randomized, double-blind, placebo-controlled, multi-center study.
Setting: Outpatient.
Patients: A total of 345 patients aged 1 to 52 years with moderate to severe dry, itchy eyes.
Interventions: Patients were randomized to receive one drop per day of Eye Lubricant or placebo for a total of 21 days.
Measurements: Patient eye comfort.
Results: The patients receiving Eye Lubricant daily reported eye comfort within 48 hours. The patients receiving placebo reported no improvement in eye comfort.
Conclusion: In this well-controlled, 21 day study, Eye Lubricant was shown to be more effective than placebo in symptom relief for moderate to severe dry, itchy eyes. Less than 1% of patients needed continual use.

Sample Package Insert (PI)

This is a fictional PI sheet for teaching purposes only. Any information that reflects a marketed product is coincidental

---

XYZ Eye Drops

Eye Lubricant
Prescribing information as of December, 2004

FOR OPTHAMALIC USE ONLY

Description
XYZ Eye Drops contain eye lubricant, a solution for optical use.

Chemical Name: Eye Lubricant.

Contains: XYZ ingredients

Registry No. XXXXXX

Clinical Pharmacology
In common with other lubricants, Eye Lubricant has moisturizing properties.

Pharmacokinetics
The extent of absorption is determined by many factors. However, there was no systemic accumulation over time.

INDICATIONS AND USAGE
XYZ Eye Drops are a lubricant for relief of medium to extra dry eyes. *XYZ Eye Drops* may be used in pediatric patients 1 year of age or older. The safety and efficacy of drug use for longer than 3 weeks has not been established.

WARNINGS:
Use only as directed.

CONTRAINDICATIONS
XYZ Eye Drops are contraindicated in those patients with a history of hypersensitivity to any of the components in its preparations.

Sample Package Insert (page 2)

PRECAUTIONS
General
If irritation develops, _XYZ Eye Drops_ should be discontinued.
If a favorable response does not occur promptly, use of _XYZ Eye Drops_ should be discontinued.
The following test may be helpful in evaluating patients: ABC Test.

Carcinogenesis, Mutagenesis, and Impairment of Fertility
Animal tests demonstrated no effect on fertility.
Pregnancy: Teratogenic Effects: Pregnancy Category B.
Eye Lubricant has not been shown to be teratogenic in laboratory animals.
Nursing Mothers
Eye Lubricant has not been shown to appear in human milk.
Pediatric Use
XYZ Eye Drops may be used in pediatric patients 1 year of age or older. Safety and efficacy of the drug use longer than 3 weeks has not been established. The use of _XYZ Eye Drops_ is supported by results from three well-controlled clinical trials in 67 pediatric patients with dry eye between the ages of 4 months and 12 years of age.

ADVERSE REACTIONS
In well-controlled clinical trials, a total of 345 patients were treated with _XYZ Eye Drops_. Treatment related adverse events were reported in 2% of the patients. Frequently reported adverse events included headache and burning, which occurred in 1% of the patients.
OVERDOSAGE
(See Precautions)
DOSAGE AND ADMINISTRATION
Apply 1 drop to each eye once daily.
HOW SUPPLIED
XYZ Eye Drops are supplied in
30 mL dropper
Store between 41 and 77F (5 and 25C).
Rx Only
Prescribing information as of December, 2004.
U.S. Patent No. XXXX
Manufactured for: ABC Pharmaceuticals   **ABC Pharmaceuticals**

Clinical Paper Worksheet

Author(s):

Publication:

Date:

Study Design:

Number of Patients:

Results/Discussion:

Key Selling Points:

Sample Ninety Day Plan Of Action

First 30 days

- ❖ Begin home study
- ❖ Meet with trainer to review training schedule
- ❖ Confirm receipt of all materials
- ❖ Review administrative information with trainer—important names and phone numbers, DM expectations, paperwork (expense reports, etc.)
- ❖ Begin reading product modules
- ❖ Take self-assessment quizzes
- ❖ Review marketing messages and clinical information with trainer
- ❖ Role-play sales call using detail piece with trainer
- ❖ Work with trainer in trainer's territory
- ❖ Prepare for Home Office training

Second 30 days

- ❖ Attend Home Office training
- ❖ Analyze territory in terms of geography, opportunity, influence, strengths and weaknesses
- ❖ Identify key opinion leaders and key prescribers
- ❖ Make calls on all high prescribers
- ❖ Schedule appointments with prescribers as required
- ❖ Meet with field counterparts to set up territory call schedule
- ❖ Learn managed care reimbursement and formulary status for products
- ❖ Work with trainer in my territory

Third 30 days

- ❖ Partner with field counterparts and trainer on identifying focus list of prescribers
- ❖ Work with territory team mates to set up a territory educational program
- ❖ Develop strategy for increasing market share for territory
- ❖ Target top 15 prescribers for increased call frequency
- ❖ Track progress
- ❖ Master managed care reimbursement and formulary status

Resources

Café Pharma www.cafepharma.com

This is the website that pharmaceutical sales professionals use the most. It offers lots of great information including company boards, industry news, classifieds, articles and rep tools. You'll find the chat rooms valuable to get a tell-it-like-it-is look at the realities of being a pharmaceutical sales rep. On the company research pages you can link to individual companies you are researching for an interview.

Corey Nahman www.coreynahman.com

This site offers the latest pharmaceutical news, professional journals and links to job sites. There is something for everyone from pharmaceutical marketers to researchers to scholars to clinicians and students. Topics covered include marketing, sales and clinical news.

Pharmaceutical Information For You www.pharmainfo.net

This site offers up-to-date clinical and regulatory information. You'll find articles, news flashes and pharmacist's information. Plus, there is a pharmacist's chat room. You can even keep up with what's happening at the FDA, follow approvals for new drugs and generics, keep up on approvals for NDA's (new drug applications), and drug recalls.

Repworkshop.com www.repworkshop.com

A website developed by the authors offering an online workshop based on the *Learn The Secrets* approach with downloadable workbook and online tutorial. You'll be able to develop your own strategy and tactics for breaking into pharmaceutical sales, as well as develop your own resume based on the principles outlined in the book and workshop.

HealthCare Business Women's Association (HBA)
www.hbanet.org

HBA is an organization dedicated to advancing the role and impact of women in healthcare. HBA offers educational programs, networking and many other professional benefits. There are chapters throughout the country, so you can locate the one nearest you through the website. Professionals attending the programs are from pharmaceutical, biotech, and healthcare industry as well as vendors that offer services to pharmaceutical companies.

Certified Medical Representative Institute
www.cmrinstitute.org

CMR is an independent, non-profit organization that sets the standard for continuing medication education, professional development and certification. CMR provides over 40 self-study courses in topics ranging from science and medicine to business and pharmaceutical management. The course work will help speed up your learning curve once you land your job.

St. Joseph's Haub School of Business, Philadelphia, PA
www.sju.edu

St. Joseph's offers an undergraduate Pharmaceutical Marketing degree as well as an Executive Pharmaceutical Marketing MBA. The undergraduate program is an interdisciplinary experience grounded in liberal arts and combining business with a focus on the pharmaceutical industry. This program prepares students for positions in sales, marketing, market research and other jobs at pharmaceutical companies. It has partnerships with all major pharmaceutical companies placing undergraduates with summer internships as well as full time positions after graduation.

Pharmaceutical Representative Magazine www.pharmrep.com

The only newsmagazine designed solely for the pharmaceutical sales representative. The newsmagazine offers everything from sales tips to what our peers are doing to what's happening on the political scene, such as drug re-importation.

Pharmaceutical Executive Magazine www.pharmexec.com

The magazine executives are reading that offers the latest on everything from marketing to sales. Have you ever wondered what marketing and sales survey your manager is quoting numbers from? It's probably from something he or she read in Pharmaceutical Executive Magazine.

Pharmaceutical Research and Manufacturers of America PhRMA www.phrma.org

This is the industry's trade association. You can download a copy of the new marketing code on interactions with healthcare providers. Pharmaceutical companies have agreed to abide by these guidelines and sales representatives are held accountable.

Acknowledgments

Learn The Secrets grew out of individual coaching and group workshops that the authors were doing independently with clients who wanted to break into pharmaceutical sales. When we started putting together our ideas, to our surprise and delight, we had an approach that made a big difference for people who wanted to position themselves effectively and leap all the hurdles of the interview process in breaking into pharmaceutical sales.

We owe special thanks to the many pharmaceutical executives, representatives, district managers and regional managers who shared their insights and stories of breaking into the business with us. Thank you all, but special thanks to Ellen Weller, Joan Shisler, Troy Bishop, Nate Joy, Mary Darrell, Steve Goodstein, Eileen Ulrich, Josie Flynn and Sandy Evans. We owe a great debt to Sandy Evans who carefully read over the sections on clinical issues and the sample sales pieces we developed for our fictional *XYZ Eye Drops*. Our thanks also to Roberta Maguire for copy-editing the manuscript, Jim Hennessy for reading the manuscript, and Janet Smoot for final graphics and formatting.

Catherine owes extraordinary thanks to her husband, Mike, and son, Ramsey, for their love and support throughout this project, and to her cousin and friend, Gary Gulkis, who is her mentor on all writing endeavors.

Lynn owes thanks to her family, especially her mother, Barbara, who has provided a lifetime of love and encouragement and son, Jim for his continued love and support throughout this project, and to all of her district managers who contributed to her successful career as a pharmaceutical sales representative and trainer.

Tell Us Your Story

We would love to hear from you about your own success in landing a job as a pharmaceutical sales representative. Tell us how you did it and what's working on sales calls with prescribers in today's dynamic and competitive selling environment.

Write or email us and let us know what worked for you on your job hunt and the experiences you had in the interview and job search process. Share with us where you'd like to see improvement in the process. Let us know how we might be able to help people like yourself better. Specifically:

❖ How did you land your first job in pharmaceutical sales?

❖ What tips can you offer new candidates trying to break into pharmaceutical sales?

❖ What was your initial experience like on the job?

❖ What was your biggest surprise in the job hunt? On the job?

❖ What innovative sales approaches or solutions were effective?

Your insights will be helpful to the next generation of pharmaceutical sales reps.

If you'd like to explore an online workshop or get information on workshops near where you live on *Learn The Secrets*, visit <u>www.repworkshop.com</u>.

Repworkshop.com
336 Central Park West #8F
New York, NY 10025-7111

Send your stories and comments to:
    stories@repworkshop.com
    catherine@selfbrand.com
    lynn@pharmamindshare.com

About The Authors

Catherine Kaputa is a career coach and personal branding strategist and the founder of SelfBrand LLC. In her coaching, Catherine works with people who are smart, talented and ambitious, and who want to leverage brand strategy to compete in a dynamic, competitive marketplace. Catherine uses the branding strategies and principles from the commercial world to help clients develop a winnable position that will set them apart and create demand. Many of her clients have "rebranded" themselves to enter new careers or launch businesses, including people who became successful pharmaceutical sales representatives. Catherine is a frequent speaker on personal branding and is also an assistant adjunct professor at New York University, Stern School of Business. For fifteen years, Catherine was SVP, Director of Advertising and Community Affairs at Smith Barney, where she led global advertising and branding initiatives. Catherine has also worked at Wells, Rich Greene and Trout & Ries Advertising. For more information, visit www.selfbrand.com or email Catherine@selfbrand.com

Lynn Zimmerman is the founder and president of Pharma Mindshare LLC, a sales training and consulting company focused on the pharmaceutical industry. Lynn has an extensive background in the industry: she has worked as a sales representative, a sales trainer and business development specialist. For fourteen years with a major pharmaceutical company, Lynn Zimmerman worked with executive staff, managers, and representatives as she helped train sales forces, led business development efforts, and acted as team leader for a major drug. As a sales representative trainer, she focused on the marketing of and the science behind pharmaceutical products. She worked with individual representatives, as well as select teams, in the primary care and specialty markets. In addition to her sales training and consulting work, Lynn is a frequent speaker in the pharmaceutical industry and leads workshops for new and seasoned sales reps. She is also a guest lecturer at St. Joseph's University. For more information, visit www.pharmamindshare.com or email lynn@pharmamindshare.com

978-0-595-34164-1
0-595-34164-0

Printed in the United States
30002LVS00004B/412

9 780595 341641